STRAYS, THE MUSICAL!

A Drama-dy
In Two Acts

CONTACT:

Amy Shojai, CABC
PO Box 1904
Sherman TX 75091
Amy@shojai.com
903-868-1022

Frank Steele
430 West Belden
Sherman TX 75090
The.steeles@verizon.net
903-893-2039

STRAYS, the MUSICAL

DIRECTOR'S NOTES

STRAYS, THE MUSICAL is written especially with pet lovers in mind and explores furry foibles from the PETS' point of view. The actors give voice to a variety of cat and dog characters in this hilarious and often moving "drama-dy" that seeks to edu-tain audiences about normal pet behavior while honoring the bond we share with pets. The complete show runs approximately two hours with an intermission. It can be performed with or without a break.

STRAYS is a review format show, with a mix of funny to poignant scenes (with and without music) designed to be modular. That is, it can be licensed for performance using only the cat-specific, dog-specific or general (both) content that best suits the audience. The authors hope it will be widely used in pet-specific fund-raising efforts.

CASTING NOTES

STRAYS can be cast with any age performer, but age 14 to adult is recommended. It is important that actors have at least like pets—this empathy is vital to the success of the show and cannot be faked. Actors can be encouraged to create their own cat/dog characters based on the scenes/songs they will perform, including "naming" their characters to replace generic names when not otherwise specified. The **PARIAH CAT**, **PUPPY** and **KITTEN** characters remain constant throughout the show; other actors may create a different character in each scene, as you wish. This is an ensemble show, with no specific "stars" and all actors onstage throughout the performance.

A mix of body types, ages and genders offers the most fun and flexibility, as well as reflecting the message that pets also come in all shapes, sizes, personalities, ages and looks. The "type" of character (dog or cat, specific breed, young or old, etc.) should come primarily from the actor's actions and cued from the dialogue.

The show can be mounted with as few as **EIGHT ADULT SINGER/ACTORS** doubling roles, or **25+ FEATURED PLAYERS** plus a **CHORUS** that may include young performers as puppies and kittens. Suggested casting/doubling recommendations follow, but songs and scenes may be mixed and matched to best fit talents.

CHARACTER BREAKDOWNS:

PARIAH CAT (Female/Alto): A haunted soul shunned by all, she starts the show with her solo opening of STRAYS, delivers the heartbreaking I LIVE BY NIGHT monologue, a hopeful modern dance solo in DREAM CAT, finds love in LEAST OF THESE and sings celebratory solo/trio in RAINBOW PETS.

PUPPY (Male or Female/Alto): Clueless 12-week-old cutie, everything's fun and games. Specific features include PUPPY MONOLOGUE, INNAPROPRIATE PET GIFTS, PUFF PUFF, TV'd scene and others, and solo in GOTCHA DAY. May double **SWAGGER** if versatile adult male actor is cast.

SWAGGER (Male/Tenor): Think teen heartthrob, performs ITCHY DOG solo. He may double to perform **DOG RAPPER** in NORMAL, as well as egotistical SHOW DOG monologue. May double **PUPPY**.

KITTEN (Female/Soprano): Mostly wide-eyed innocent but can be feisty, and has bouncing-off-the-wall energy. She shares the touching DREAM CAT echo duet (soprano to high F), is backup trio singer in GRAZING, performs in PUFF PUFF, TV'd scene and others, and rallies the rest of the pets in solos in GOTCHA DAY. She may double the "top-cat" **TRIO** in NORMAL rap.

HOUND DOG (Male/Bass): Broad comic relief in GRAZING (bass to low A), and bombastic fun in the PET DEBATE and NORMAL scene. He may double the part of **BASSET**.

BASSET (Male): Non-singing role ranges from sadly resigned VO in IT'S TIME, to knee-slapping comedy as the deaf dog in OLD DOGS TALKING. If a singer, may double **HOUND DOG**.

MOM-CAT (Female): Non-singing no-nonsense motherly character offers deadpan contrast to balance other flamboyant characters. She's featured in GRAZING scene and DODGING THE BULLET. If a singer, actress can also double as **PRACTICAL CAT**.

PRACTICAL CAT (Female/2nd Soprano): Smart, intolerant of idiots whether cats or dogs, and has a teasing nature. Featured in the PUFF-PUFF scene, solos in NORMAL including "top cat" and RAINBOW PETS **TRIO**. May double **MOM-CAT**.

QUEEN CAT (Female/Soprano): Regal, opinionated and bossy, she IS the QUEEN CAT (in her opinion—and that's all that matters). Features include PET DEBATE and the hopeful DREAM CAT (soprano to high F). Actress may double **DEBATE CAT** and/or **GOSPEL CAT**.

DEBATE CAT (Female): Non-singing sophisticated, condescending, whips doggy butt in arguing the "cat side" in the PET DEBATE scene. If a singer, may double **QUEEN CAT** or **NOBODY'S CAT**.

GOSPEL CAT (Female/Soprano): Stylish sleek feline who comforts and encourages all she meets, and "testifies" to all about how cats and dogs inspire humans in THE MUSE. May double **TRIO** to sing backup/features in GRAZING, NORMAL, 8 LIVES IN HEAVEN and RAINBOW PETS. May double **QUEEN CAT**.

BLUESY DOG (Female/Alto or Male/Baritone): A lovable clueless pooch featured in CUZ I'M A DAWG solo. May double to sing (treble) backup on 8 LIVES IN HEAVEN, and the heartbreaking **NOBODY'S DOG**.

PETER NAPOLEON (Male): Non-singing role. Small and hairy but big dog attitude, straight man in comedy scenes which include DODGING THE BULLET and INNAPROPRIATE PET GIFTS. If a singer, may double **CHIHUAHUA**.

CHIHUAHUA (Male/Tenor): Nervous and shaky, may speak with an accent, featured in PUFF PUFF, solos in NORMAL, and featured in OLD DOGS TALKING. May double **PETER NAPOLEON**.

MUTT (Male/Baritone): Performs poignant VO in IT'S TIME, sings the haunting folk solo DOG ON THE RUN, (to low A-flat, but may be sung up an octave). May double **DOBERMAN**.

DOBERMAN (Male): Non-singing comic character, an old dog living in the past, may speak with German accent, featured in OLD DOGS TALKING. If a singer, may double **MUTT.**

LUCKY CAT (Male): Non-singing accident prone, funny, bumbling, but can break hearts with his earnest wish for love. His features include talk-sung EIGHT LIVES IN HEAVEN, DODGING THE BULLET. May double **CAT RAPPER,** and if a singer, may double **PUFF PUFF** and/or **NOBODY'S CAT**.

PUFF PUFF (Male/Tenor or Female/Alto): A cat the "size of a Volvo" with defensive posturing attitude. Nothing is ever his/her fault. Featured in PUFF PUFF scene with solo verses in NORMAL. May be doubled by **LUCKY CAT**.

GLAMOUR DOG (Female/Alto): Style-conscious Calypso-dancing Poodle. She sings backup trio in GRAZING, and is featured in ITCHY DOG scene and dance, and OLD DOGS TALKING. May double **OFFSTAGE VO 2**.

OFFSTAGE VO 1 (Male/Baritone): Doubles as **OLD GRUFF** in IT'S TIME and **OWNER 2** in NOBODY'S DOG and various "dog" characters as needed. Features include THE LEAST OF THESE.

OFFSTAGE VO 2 (Female/Soprano): May double **GLAMOUR DOG**, as well as **OWNER 1** in NOBODY'S DOG with solos/features include THE LEAST OF THESE. May double RAINBOW PETS **TRIO.**

CAT RAPPER and **DOG RAPPER (Male or Female):** D'ogmatic delivery with c'attitude plus, these swaggering actors are featured in the NORMAL song. A minimum of two should be cast, but the rap lyrics can be shared between several actors. (May be doubled by **LUCKY CAT** and **SWAGGER**.)

NOBODY'S DOG and **NOBODY'S CAT (Male/Tenor and Female/Alto):** Heartbreaking delivery that echoes IT'S TIME scene yet offers hope in the PERFECT scene. Also sings solos in LEAST OF THESE. May be doubled by **LUCKY CAT** and **BLUESY DOG**.

TRIO (Females): Three (or more) cat-girls able to sing close harmony while performing simple choreography. They sing backup on GRAZING, the NORMAL "top cat" during rap, melody and descant on 8 LIVES IN HEAVEN and featured trio/cannon in show-stopping RAINBOW PETS. Different actresses may perform each song, or the same three sing on all features. May be doubled by other strong singers in cast such as **GOSPEL CAT, KITTEN, MOM-CAT, PRACTICAL-CAT** and/or **QUEEN CAT**.

CHORUS (Male/Female as needed): Performs company songs/dances, and group or solo lines as needed in the songs STRAYS, NORMAL, THE MUSE, GOTCHA DAY, LEAST OF THESE and RAINBOW PETS. Think about casting "puppy/kitten chorus" to sing the chorus verses of NORMAL, for instance. Additional **OWNERS** (parents of these young actors) may be cast to "adopt" them in the LEAST OF THESE scene.

STRAYS, the MUSICAL

SCENES, SETTINGS & MUSICAL NUMBERS

Act 1

Scene 1 (Outside) *Strays*..Company

Scene 2 (Cage) Puppy Monologue ....Pup

Scene 3 (Shelter) *Grazing* ....Hound, Mom, Glamour, Kitten

Scene 4 (Outside) I Live By Night..Pariah

Scene 5 (Shelter) *Itchy Dog*...............................Swagger, Glamour

Scene 6 (Cage) Pet Debate, *Dream Cat*.......Hound, Queen, Kitten, Pariah

Scene 7 (Shelter) Dodging The Bullet........Mom, Napol, Pup, Lucky, Kit

Scene 8 (Blackout) It's Time......................Gruff, VO2, Dobie, Basset

Scene 9 (Shelter) *Cuz I'm A Dawg*........................Bluesy, Kit, Swagger

Scene 10 (Shelter) Puff Puff, *Normal*.........................Company, VO1

Act 2

Scene 1 (Outside) *Dog On The Run*...Mutt

Scene 2 (Alley) Show Dog...Swagger, VO2

Scene 3 (Alley) Inappropriate Pet Gifts..........................Napol, Pup

Scene 4 (Outside) *Eight Lives In Heaven*.................Puff, Queen, Bluesy

Scene 5 (Alley) Old Dogs Talking.............Basset, Chi, Dobie, Glamour

Scene 6 (Blackout/Shelter) Furry Gifts, *Muse*......VO2, Gospel, Ensemble

Scene 7 (Shelter) TV'd, *Gotcha Day*.......................Kitten, Pup, Company

Scene 8 (Shelter) Nobody's Dog/Cat..............................Owners 1 & 2

Scene 9 (Shelter) Perfect, *Least Of These* ...Nobody's Dog/Cat, Company

Scene 10 (Shelter) Pick of The Litter, *Rainbow Pets*......Pariah, Company

Curtain Call, *Strays Reprise*..Company

PRODUCTION HISTORY:

Selected songs and scenes from **STRAYS, the MUSICAL!** were first produced and directed by Amy Shojai and Frank Steele in a preview performance at Trinity Lutheran Church, Sherman Texas on October 27, 2013, and performed again in Dallas, Texas on November 1, 2013 at the 20th Annual Cat Writers Association Conference. The preview cast included Amy Shojai, Gil Nelson, Theresa Littlefield, Suellen Davis, and Frank Steele.

A staged reading of the completed **STRAYS** show was performed March 22, 2014 at the Honey McGee Playhouse, 313 West Mulberry Street, Sherman, TX 75090 in conjunction with Theatricks/Sherman Community Players. The cast of Amy Shojai, Gil Nelson, Diana Adair, Aaron Adair, Johnny Flowers and Frank Steele also recorded an album of the 12 STRAYS songs, produced by Jim Barnes Audio Productions. This **STRAYS Cast Recording** currently is available for free listening at http://tinyurl.com/l4y8r5w

STRAYS, THE MUSICAL full production was first staged and performed November 6, 7, 8, 2014 at the Honey McGee Playhouse with the following cast. View a sample from the opening night performance here, http://youtu.be/nru88uGiV7w.

PARIAH CAT	Kaitlyn Casmedes
PUPPY	Kate Carson
SWAGGER/NOBODY'S DOG	Jessie Childress
KITTEN	Sarah McGinn
HOUND DOG/BASSET	Lew Cohn
MOM-CAT(I.3)	Charlotte Thompson
MOM-CAT/PRACTICAL CAT	Marty Burkart
DEBATE CAT/NOBODY'S CAT	Susan McGinn
QUEEN CAT/OWNER 1	Christina Childress
GOSPEL CAT	MacKenzie Kozak
BLUESY DOG/DOG RAP	Theresa Littlefield
PETER NAPOLEON/CHIHUAHUA	Steve Mildward
MUTT/DOBERMAN	Ken Kozak
LUCKY CAT/PUFF PUFF/RAP CAT	Jim Barnes
GLAMOUR DOG/OWNER 6	Katie Wiley
VO 1/OLD GRUFF/OWNER 2	John McGinn
VO 2/OWNER 3	Carolina Guerra
VO (Furry Gifts)	Ava Gibson
VO YOUNG VOICE/FAST RAP	Kevin Gautier

CHORUS: Sophia Allen, Abraham Guerra, Eliana Guerra, Sofia Guerra, Avery Hall, Brenna Michaelsen, Brynn Riley, Charity Riley, Liam Troncalli, Sofia Westmoreland

PRODUCTION STAFF

Directors	Amy Shojai, Frank Steele
Music Director	Amy Shojai
Technical Advisor	Steven Mildward
Stage Managers	Brenna Michaelsen, Tobias Scheibmeir
Rehearsal Pianist	John McGinn
Choreographer	Kaitlyn Casmedes
Costumes	Company
Hair/Makeup	Katie Wiley & Roxy Farrell
Light Design/Operator	Tom Rawson
Spotlight Operator	Michael Gardner
Sound Technician	Jim Barnes
Audio/Video Design	Amy Shojai

Set Design/Construction: Webster Crocker, John Lonnevik, Frank Steele, Steven Mildward, Amy Shojai

VOCAL AND MOVEMENT REQUIREMENTS

Music consists of a variety of song styles from pop to blues to gospel. The multiple verses offer lots of feature solo line opportunities. Solo numbers may have backup singers, and company numbers require two- to three-part harmonies. Most songs are easy mid-range tenor and alto lines.

Harmony mostly is written as "rounds" or combinations of two or three melody lines. This keeps learning music simple for non-music-readers. A piano score for rehearsal is available, with show performance using a CD with full orchestration; a rehearsal piano/vocal CD can be provided. Vocal ranges from baritone (from low A-flat) to soprano (to high F). A cast recording is available to demonstrate recommended performance voicing.

Strong dance ability is not required. Movement that enhances cat and dog characters and personalities is encouraged. Fun, campy choreography particularly of backup singers as in GRAZING, and company production numbers (NORMAL and GOTCHA DAY) enhance the production.

COSTUMES, PROPS/SET PIECES/STAGING (general)

Costumes and props should suggest the character, such as dog collars, squeaky dog toys, balls, cat feather wands and the like. Do not dress actors in "dog/cat suits" or use pet-centric makeup. Minimal suggestions may be used—furry "sleeves" or leggings, or ponytails with bows for dog "ears" for example, in dog/cat colors and patterns. The show primarily must rely on the actors' skills to bring the animal characters to life. A costume "cue" that identifies cats from dogs may be helpful, such as dog bone pendants or cat bells. OWNERS in last scene should by contrast wear bright colors, skirts, and non-pet-looking hair styles.

The show can be performed on a bare stage with actors entering/exiting from and interacting with the audience. Area lighting and minimal set pieces, such as garbage cans, door frame, cage bars (physical or with lights) should be enough to suggest three distinct spaces: **OUTDOORS**, next to an **ALLEY** and **SHELTER**. Multiple levels with oversize boxes, dog beds, trees etc. (scaled to actor-pet size) may also be effective for "shelter" scenes. Video projections incorporated into the performance of "real" cats and dogs, shelter settings or other artistic uses may also enhance the performance. IT'S TIME and THE MUSE performance videos are available.

ACT I

Scene 1, STRAYS

> *The action of the play opens OUTDOORS. Actors appear from back of the theater house and enter stage from various positions from audience. PARIAH CAT enters first, frightened, watching audience, suspicious and fearful.*
>
> *STRAYS music begins and PARIAH sings first lines, each section of lyric cues the entrances, with each actor adding his/her voice to the song as each enters until full company takes the stage.*

(PARIAH)
I'M JUST A STRAY
RUNNING ON MY OWN,
LOOKIN' FOR A WAY HOME,
A PLACE TO STAY.

(NOBODY'S DOG)
ON MY WAY,
FUN AND GAMES ON LOAN,
BOOKIN' IT ALONE
FOR ONE MORE DAY.

(NOBODY'S CAT)
WHY CAN'T YOU SEE?
WON'T YOU LOOK AT ME?

(ALL)
FREEDOM'S NOT FOR FREE.
ANYTHING, I'LL DO.
ALL I CAN GIVE

I'LL LIVE THE WAY YOU LIVE.
ANYTHING FORGIVE
SHARE MY LIFE WITH YOU.

NEVER HAD A HOME, NO ONE TO LOVE,
I'M ON A SEARCH FOR AN OPENING DOOR.
CAN'T WAIT TO SEE WHAT'S MEANT TO BE,
WHAT D'YA SAY? MAYBE TODAY?

Following lines are spoken as MUSIC continues underneath.

ALL
I was born to love you.

DOG 1
I'm shaggy, shorthair, big, small, and all different colors.

DOG 2
For a pat on the rump, or a scratch behind the ear, I'll do anything for you.

CAT 1
Pet me, and I'll purr. Then I'll attack your hand.

CAT 2
Leave on a trip and I'll pretend it doesn't matter, and hiss to hide the hurt.

PUPPY
If you're rich, we'll live well.

KITTEN
If you're poor, we'll live day by day. But it won't matter if we're together.

DOG 1
I'll protect you to the death because I'm your dog, and I have a job to do. I'll lick clean your tears of sadness.

CAT 1
And I'll play the clown to make you smile.

CAT 2
I'll purr when I'm happy, and I'll purr when I'm hurt.

DOG 2
I'll wag my tail each and every time I see you to show how important you are to me.

KITTEN

I'm hated because I'm a cat. I'm feared because I'm a cat. I'm loved because I'm a cat.

PUPPY

The life you have chosen is my life, too. I'm not only your dog, most importantly, I'm your friend.

CAT 1

I chose you as much as you chose me. I am your cat, and you are my person. I'm a reflection of you.

ALL

We are partners for life.

(ALL SING)

I WANT A HOME, SOMEONE TO LOVE.
WHEN LEFT IN THE LURCH, I WON'T EVEN THE SCORE.
FATED TO BE, IF YOU'LL JUST TAKE ME
NO MORE A STRAY, COME WHAT MAY.

I'M JUST A STRAY
RUNNING ON MY OWN,
LOOKIN' FOR A WAY HOME,
A PLACE TO STAY.

ON MY WAY,
FUN AND GAMES ON LOAN,
BOOKIN' IT ALONE
FOR ONE MORE DAY.

EYES SAY IT ALL.
LOVE THAT'S NEVER SMALL
JUST A WHISPERED CALL
TELLS ME YOU WILL TRY.
WILL YOU HEAR MY HEART?
IS THIS WHERE WE START,
NEVER TO DEPART?
WON'T YOU HEAR MY CRY?
PLEASE, PLEASE PLEASE
HEAR MY CRY.

Blackout.

Scene 2, PUPPY MONOLOGUE

Area lights up on PUPPY.

PUPPY

So, I'm in the pet store window, watching kids making faces at me, dancing around trying to dodge my own poop, you know...being cute, when this woman comes in. She a big one, too. Looks a little like a beach ball with arms, and I swear, she's singing, "How Much Is That Doggie In The window?" I'm thinking to myself, "Oh, please...not this one. Maybe she's looking at the other window." Well, I look over, and in the other window is a python, so I know she's zeroing in on me.

Well, I'm saying to myself, "OK...I can go with this one. If she's, let's say...portly, maybe she's pretty generous with the feedbag." That might not be bad, and it's gotta be better than gravel they feed me here. So, she picks me up, makes cooing noises right in my face and pays the guy. I'm headed to a new home!

When I get there, it's pretty sweet. A new doggie bed, some nice wet food, a pan of fresh water...yep, I'm gonna like it here. Then comes the rub. "I'd like you to meet Mr. Puff Puff," she says. Mr. Puff Puff is this cat the size of a Volvo and he takes a swipe at me. Luckily I dodge him, but it's hate at first sight. This creep has claws the size of eagle talons, and he looks at me like I'm his next meal. Note to myself: GIVE MR. PUFF PUFF A WIDE BERTH!!

Things go along pretty well for the first few days, then comes the naming process. "I'll call you Dinky," she says, which soon morphs into 'Dunkums,' 'Dinkydo,' 'Dinkles,' and my least favorite...'Dinkydoodle.' Well, what are ya gonna do? Every time I respond to any of the new names I get a treat, so I play along.

See, it's not easy being the new puppy. You hafta go through the new trick procedures. First up was 'fetching the slippers.' Now, these things smelled like old Swiss cheese. Did I say "Old?" I mean ancient! maybe from the first batch ever made. Anyway, I did it. Why? Because I got a treat. Next was 'fetching the paper.' Rain, hail, sleet, or snow, there I was running out like Jesse Owens grabbing a paper that the goofball paper boy tossed in the trees, the flower bed, the grass, the driveway, over the septic tank. I want to say, "Hey, Helen Keller...take aim once in a while. I'm tired of being a mind reader and guessing where you're gonna throw it next." And...again, I did it. Why? Say it with me this time. "Because I got a treat."

Treats are important to a guy(girl) like me. In fact, I delayed my own house-training because the more accidents I had, and the more I got it right, I got a treat.

I heard my person say that I'm going to get fixed! Now, I'm not exactly sure what that is, but if there's a treat involved, it's gotta be good. I'm looking forward to it. Fixed. Yeah, I can go with it. I'm gonna get a treat!

Lights fade out on PUPPY.

Scene 3, GRAZING

Lights fade in on SHELTER. MOM-CAT is pawing under bathroom door, with KITTEN. DOGS join him/her.

GLAMOUR DOG

What are you doing?

MOM-CAT

It's locked. I gotta get in there!

HOUND DOG

But…your litter box is over there. (*Has litter on nose.*)

MOM-CAT

You don't understand. (*Singing to the tune of* CHICAGO, MY KIND OF TOWN *a la Frank Sinatra*) My kinda place, the bathroom is. . .

HOUND DOG

Oh, I get that. Nothing unexpected in there. Something you can always count on. I know what you mean.

MOM-CAT

In my old place—you know, before I strayed—used to head for the potty place first thing in the morning to get a fresh sip from that gi-normous water bowl. Cool, fresh, always available. And when the lid was down, I'd just hop up on the sink, slurp from the faucet while SHE was doing her own thing, get some scritches and head bonks. *(sigh).* Routine, how I love routine! Best time of the day, I tell ya.

GLAMOUR DOG

Yeah, belly up to the doggy watering hole. I hear you!

                        HOUND DOG
In my old place, before I left, I lived under the porch, dodging spiders, hoping snakes didn't show up. And when it rained it was a huge puddle of mud. When the porch collapsed, I was out of there.

                        MOM-CAT
Oh, you poor mud-puppy, you were one of those porch dogs. Me, spiders in the house are always value added. At my old place, the sink was legal. It was the countertop cruising got my people hissed off. (*Glares at Dog 2*) At least the OUTSIDE dogs never messed with my personal space. (*Whispers explanation to KITTEN*)

                        KITTEN
You're kidding. That can't be right. (*To DOG 1*) Why would you ever even think of trying such a thing?

                        GLAMOUR-DOG
Trying what?

                        HOUND DOG
(*Whispers to DOG 1*)

> *They speak the following lines as music to* <u>GRAZING</u> *begins.*

                        GLAMOUR-DOG
You're kidding. Really, it's that tasty?

                        HOUND DOG
Trust me, those cats waste way too much nutrition. The second time around is great, and the smell can't be beat.

> *MOM-CAT, KITTEN and GLAMOUR-DOG (or alternate TRIO) sing "poop-she-waddy" lines with choreographed campy backup singer moves while using litter scoopers like microphones. HOUND DOG sings solo in an Elvis delivery style.*

    POOP-SHE-WADDY-WADDY
    POOP-SHE-WADDY-WADDY
    POOP-SHE-WADDY-WADDY
    POOP-SHE-WADDY-WADDY

LITTER BOX GRAZING, DANG, IT'S MIGHTY GOOD.

    POOP-SHE-WADDY-WADDY
    POOP-SHE-WADDY-WADDY

SHOULDN'TA DONE IT, BUT DID IT CUZ I COULD.

    POOP-SHE-WADDY-WADDY
    POOP-SHE-WADDY-WADDY

ATE IT ALL UP, AND THERE IT WENT.
PASS THE MOUTHWASH, OR A BIG BREATH MINT.
CUZ I'M GRAZING.

    POOP-SHE-WADDY-WADDY
    POOP-SHE-WADDY-WADDY.
    POOP-SHE-WADDY-WADDY
    POOP-SHE-WADDY-WADDY.

GET FUSSED AT FOR GRAZING, BUT WHAT ELSE CAN I DO?

    POOP-SHE-WADDY-WADDY
    POOP-SHE-WADDY-WADDY

SEE IT IN THE BOX, A BRAND NEW PILE OF POO.

    POOP-SHE-WADDY-WADDY
    POOP-SHE-WADDY-WADDY

SOON IT'S GONE, WITHOUT A TRACE.
THEN I COME AND LICK YOUR FACE.
CUZ I'M GRAZING.

    POOP-SHE-WADDY-WADDY
    POOP-SHE-WADDY-WADDY.
    POOP-SHE-WADDY-WADDY
    POOP-SHE-WADDY-WADDY.

FOLKS KEEP SAYING "I'VE GOT NO TASTE"
BUT, BRING ME A PLATE OF KITTY WASTE,
THE FASTER, THE BETTER, I MEAN POST HASTE.
CUZ I'M GRAZING.

    POOP-SHE-WADDY-WADDY
    POOP-SHE-WADDY-WADDY.

> POOP-SHE-WADDY-WADDY
> POOP-SHE-WADDY-WADDY.

NEED TO BREAK THE HABIT, TOMORROW'LL BE THE DAY.

> POOP-SHE-WADDY-WADDY
> POOP-SHE-WADDY-WADDY.

IF NOT TOMORROW, MAYBE A MONTH AWAY.

> POOP-SHE-WADDY-WADDY
> POOP-SHE-WADDY-WADDY.

GOT A MONKEY ON MY BACK, BUT IT'S NOT MY WISH.
JUST CAN'T PASS UP THOSE TOILET FISH.
CUZ I'M GRAZING.

> POOP-SHE-WADDY-WADDY
> POOP-SHE-WADDY-WADDY.
> POOP-SHE-WADDY-WADDY
> POOP-SHE-WADDY-WADDY.

WAIT A MINUTE, WHAT'S THAT? I'M NOT REAL SURE.

> POOP-SHE-WADDY-WADDY
> POOP-SHE-WADDY-WADDY.

GETTING A WHIFF OF THAT LATEST POOP DU JOUR.

> POOP-SHE-WADDY-WADDY
> POOP-SHE-WADDY-WADDY.

JUST CAN'T STOP ME, DON'T ASK WHY,
NO WAY TO STOP ME, DON'T EVEN TRY.
CUZ I'M GRAZING.

> POOP-SHE-WADDY-WADDY
> POOP-SHE-WADDY-WADDY.

EVERYONE SAYS, "I'VE GOT NO TASTE."
IT'S CALLING ME BACK, THAT KITTY WASTE.
IT'S THE WORST SITUATION I'VE EVER FACED.
I'M STILL GRAZING.

> POOP-SHE-WADDY-WADDY
> POOP-SHE-WADDY-WADDY
> POOP-SHE-WADDY-WADDY
> POOP-SHE-WADDY-WADDY

IF I HAD BETTER FOOD, THAT JUST MIGHT BE THE CURE.

> POOP-SHE-WADDY-WADDY
> POOP-SHE-WADDY-WADDY.

BUT THE LITTER BOX IS REALLY QUITE THE LURE.

> POOP-SHE-WADDY-WADDY
> POOP-SHE-WADDY-WADDY.

IF YOU WANT TO STOP MY FITS,
FEED ME SOMETHING GOOD, AND I'LL CALL IT QUITS.
NO MORE GRAZING.

> POOP-SHE-WADDY-WADDY
> POOP-SHE-WADDY-WADDY.

EVERYONE SAYS, "I'VE GOT NO TASTE."
IT'S CALLING ME BACK, THAT KITTY WASTE.
IT'S THE WORST SITUATION I'VE EVER FACED.
I'M STILL GRAZING.

> POOP-SHE-WADDY-WADDY
> POOP-SHE-WADDY-WADDY
> POOP-SHE-WADDY-WADDY-WOOOOOOO

> *Lights fade out.*

Scene 4, I LIVE BY NIGHT

> *OUTSIDE in dim moonlight, blue stage.*

PARIAH CAT

I live by night. I have to. Life during the day was a series of dodging BBs, glass bottles, and anything else that could be thrown at me. My question has always been, "Why?" Is it because my coat isn't shiny? My eyes are haunted by fear? My ears are crusty with mites?

That's the appearance. That's what everyone sees.

I look through windows and see other cats being petted, played with, and fed. I see them sleeping on cushions, in chairs, or on beds. Their eyes don't look like mine. They're safe. They're cared for. They're loved, while I eat scraps from the garbage. I'm jealous, and I envy them.

I want to be brushed, scratched under my chin, and I want someone to look at me as though he or she likes me. Is that too much to ask? Am I expecting too much? I'd trade the rest of my lives for one day like that. Maybe for one hour like that.

Here's what no one understands. There is a void in my heart waiting to be filled with love. Yet, my heart is full of love to give.

I live by night, and this night will be like all the others. Sad, seeking security, looking for food, and trying to find a warm place to sleep—the guarded sleep that I've become accustomed to.

If someone or something created all of us, please, please let me be loved. Let me show someone what I have to give, what I have to offer. Let this be the last day I have to drink from puddles in the street. Let this be the day that someone looks past my appearance, and sees what's in my heart.

I live by night....

Blackout

Scene 5: ITCHY DOG

> *Lights up on GLAMOUR-DOG and SWAGGER-PUP in SHELTER.*

SWAGGER
(Full of bravado, wanting to hear the older dog's "war" stories.) Tell me about when the porch fell down. Will ya, huh? Was it exciting? Was it noisy? Were you scared? How'd you get out? I would a dashed out of the way, you know, at the last minute. *(Dancing around, ducking and weaving, fancy paw-work.)* I'm pretty fast, you know.

GLAMOUR
Scared? Me scared? Who told you that? Nuh-huh, not me. The ground was already wet, that wasn't me. But the noise woke me out of a sound sleep, so loud it hurt my ears. One minute I had a roof over my head—so to speak—and then my world collapsed. Had to tunnel my way out. That's how I got this limp. *(Demonstrates a sexy strut.)*

SWAGGER

(*Delighted.*) You got to *dig*? You lucky dog! I love to dig, I really dig digging. And you had the perfect excuse. Nobody could blame you for excavating to escape. Wow, play and dig and get covered in mud, what fun! What did your people do?

GLAMOUR

(*Pauses*) They didn't know. They'd been gone for weeks. Don't tell anyone, I got a reputation, and it sounds better to say I left them. Hey, don't look so stricken. The neighbor kid made sure I got food every day. I liked that kid. He could sure toss a Frisbee. What an arm!

SWAGGER

Why didn't you stay?

GLAMOUR

My bum leg let me down. I was chasing a Frisbee and somebody grabbed me, tossed me in a truck, and I ended up here. (*Looks around*) Regular meals, solid roof that won't collapse, I got no complaints. Except…I miss that kid. So young fella, what's your story? Did someone leave you behind, too?

SWAGGER

Naw. I had it pretty good. Except for this obnoxious cat named Puff Puff. But after I'd been there a while, I just got this irresistible urge to hit the streets. And my voice changed. No what I mean? (suddenly romantic, puts on an exotic accent). Hey, nice tail…would ya show me your limp again? *(nudge nudge, wink wink)*

GLAMOUR

Like this? (*as* <u>ITCHY DOG</u> *music starts, GLAMOUR-DOG offers doggy version of a Calypso dance, with bone-type squeaky toys like maracas. SWAGGER sings.*)

I'M JUST A YOUNG DOGGIE ON DA PROWL.
I GOT NEW FEELINS DAT MAKE ME HOWL.
MON, DEM HORMONES *DAY MAKE ME ITCH.*
      (*Alt text: THAT I CAN'T HIDE*)
LOOKIN' FOR A WILLIN' *BITCH.*
      (*Alt text: BRIDE*)

TALL OR SHORT LADY, I DON'T CARE.
REALLY UGLY, OR MAYBE FAIR.
PUT UP A FENCE, MON, AND A GUARD.
CUZ I'LL BE BIRD-DOGGIN' IN YOUR YARD.

FLIPPY, DILLY, BILLY, BIPPY, POP.
MON, DEM FELLINS DON'T NEVER STOP.
GOT DEM FELLINS FOR DA VERY FIRST TIME.
HOW 'BOUT A PUP, OR MAYBE NINE?

(Spoken) Come back to my place, I call it the Copacabana Kennel, we have real good time. I got treats for you.

YESTERDAY, I WAS DOIN' FINE.
RUNNIN', PLAYIN', AN OCCASIONAL WHINE.
NOW DEM FEELINS GOT A HOLD ON ME.
SEEKIN' A LADY, OR MAYBE THREE.

MAYBE DIS FEELIN' IT GO AWAY.
MAYBE IT COME ANOTHER DAY.
MON, I'LL BE READY WHEN IT COME ALONG.
FEELIN' FRISKY AS I SING DIS SONG.

FLIPPY, DILLY, BILLY, BIPPY, POP.
MAN, DEM FEELINS DON'T NEVER STOP.
GOT DEM FEELINS FOR DA VERY FIRST TIME.
DON'T KNOW 'BOUT YOU, MON, BUT I'M FEELIN' FINE.

(Spoken) You heard of a lap dog? I'm a leg dog, baby! (*howls and dances with DOG 2*)

GOT SOME LADIES I'LL SEE TODAY.
BEFORE DIS FEELIN' IT GO AWAY.
HIDE YOUR POODLES AND BOXERS, TOO.
PLAN ON PITCHIN' LOTSA DOGGIE WOO.

IF YA SEE ME BETTER STAND WAY BACK.
GOT A MISSION, AND I'M RIGHT ON TRACK.
LOOKIN' FOR ANYTHING DATS WEARIN' FUR.
SO TO SPEAK, MON, AS IT WERE.

FLIPPY, DILLY, BILLY, BIPPY, POP.
MON, DEM FEELINS DON'T NEVER STOP.
GOT DEM FEELINS FOR THE VERY FIRST TIME.
DON'T KNOW 'BOUT YOU, MON, BUT I'M FEELIN FINE.

(ad lib sing different song) "To all the girls I've loved before..." I used to belong to Julio Iglesius. (PUPPY and DANCE DOG dance their way offstage.

Area lights down.

Scene 6: DOG-CAT DEBATE

ALLEY area lights up with garbage can podiums situated for one dog and one cat to debate. Remaining dogs/cats seated near each's respective champion-debater with audible boos, hisses, paw-thumps and howls of encouragement (within reason!).

DEBATE CAT
Mr. Dog, you have been accused of rolling in noxious substances and carrying the smell-iforousness home in an obnoxious manner. What exegesis do you have to say in your defense?

HOUND DOG
Say what?

DEBATE CAT
Why do you roll in stuff?

HOUND DOG
I just like the smell. What about you? You roll in catnip.

DEBATE CAT
But I don't inhale. Well I do, but that's different.

HOUND DOG
Yeah, you and Bill Clinton. What about your laundry feesis that you have?

DEBATE CAT
I think you mean fetish.

HOUND DOG
Yeah, what you said. Laundry fetish, what's up with that?

DEBATE CAT
It's warm. (*Glaring.*) And clean.

HOUND DOG
You're missing the best part. Do you know about used underwear? Do you know the charm of a week-old sock? Buried in the back yard and allowed to germinate…postulate…ruminate…you know, get gooder.

DEBATE CAT

I must inveigh the tone of this entire debate.

HOUND DOG

I think you mean envy. And yes, I'm all that! (*Looking off to the side.*) I'm winning this debate, right? Right?

DEBATE CAT

Look, squirrel! (*ALL DOGS rouse and look around, DOG 2 runs off stage*) Works every time.

HOUND DOG

(*Runs back onstage.*) I hate those fake out games. My old family did that, so I'm shopping for a new family. What's wrong with a little honesty?

DEBATE CAT

I don't know you that well. Some things are purr-sonal.

HOUND DOG

Aw c'mon, be a sport. Get to know me. Here, you can sniff my tail.

DEBATE CAT

I think I did. (*French accent*) Ammonia and eau de carrion.

HOUND DOG

Good, huh? It's been percolating…vacillating…cremating….distillating…

QUEEN CAT

Do you even know what you're saying?

HOUND DOG

No, not really. Does that matter?

QUEEN CAT

I guess not. (*yawns, stretches, settles to sleep, propping head on garbage can lid.*) I need a nap.

HOUND DOG

(*to KITTEN*) So, do we know each other good enough now? Can you tell me?

KITTEN

Tell you what?

HOUND DOG
She sure sleeps a lot. If she's so smart and refined and all, how'd she end up here? Did her owner boot 'er out?

KITTEN
No. *(pause)* Her owner died.

As music <u>DREAM CAT</u> begins, QUEEN CAT and KITTEN in spotlight, rest of stage black. Projected bars may suggest shelter cage. QUEEN sings solo, KITTEN sings echo lines. PARIAH CAT may dance solo at same time.

WHISKERS SHAKE,
CLOSED EYES BLINK
AT DREAM-MICE,
CHASING GHOSTS OF DAYS GONE BY.
NOW AWAKE,
YAWNING PINK,
GHOST PREY TURN TO DUST,
THEIR SHADOW SO SUBLIME.
USEFUL, USEFUL, USEFUL,
AS BROKEN PROMISES.

CLAWS FLEX,
PAWS STRETCH
LIKE WRISTS FROM SLEEVES.
BOW TO DUSK—MY TIME OF DAY.
TAIL BECKONS HEAVEN,
ALWAYS OPTIMISTIC.
PAW-STEPS MEASURE THE WAY:
THREE STEPS, FIVE BACK, NO MORE.
CHEEK-RUB CLAIMS DOMAIN.

MARKING SIGN,
    (Echo) MARKING SIGN
IN A CAT DESIGN.
    (Echo) IN A CAT DESIGN.
COUNTING TIME,
    (Echo) COUNTING TIME,
EACH PAW-STEP MINE.
    (Echo) EACH PAW STEP MINE.

THREE STEPS, FIVE BACK,
THREE BY FIVE I ROAM.
THREE STEPS, FIVE BACK,
'TILL I GO HOME.

ECHO'D STEP,
QUICKENED HEART.
INMATE EYES SLIT
IN SUDDEN BRIGHT.
SILHOUETTE DON'T DEPART!
PURRS CALL, **BELOVED!**
THERE, IN MY SIGHT.
PAWS SEEK,
  (Echo) PAWS SEEK
PAWS SEEK,
  (Echo) PAWS SEEK
PAWS SEEK
BELOVED COME AGAIN.
  (Echo) PLEASE RETURN TO ME.

OH! TO SHOULDER-PERCH,
NOSE-BUMP,
SHARE SECRETS.
SLEEP IN YOUR ARMS,
AND VANQUISH EVERY FROWN.
WHISKER-KISS THAT DEAR FACE,
GRAPPLE SHINS WITH PAW GRACE.
PLAY THE PART OF A CLOWN,
SHAMELESS,
  (Echo) SHAMELESS,
SHAMELESS,
  (Echo) SHAMELESS,
SHAMELESS,
FOR LAUGHTER'S SWEET REWARD.
  (Echo) SMILE AGAIN FOR ME.

MARKING SIGN,
  (Echo) MARKING SIGN,
IN A CAT DESIGN.
  (Echo) IN A CAT DESIGN.
COUNTING TIME,
  (Echo) COUNTING TIME,
EACH PAW-STEP MINE.
  (Echo) EACH PAW-STEP MINE.

THREE STEPS, FIVE BACK,
THREE BY FIVE I ROAM.
THREE STEPS, FIVE BACK,
PLEASE TAKE ME HOME.

LIGHTS DIE.
DOOR CLOSED.
FOOTSTEPS FADE AWAY,
BUT HOPE SHALL STAY.
OTHERS CRY, WHILE I DOZE,
PAWS CLEAN GRIEF
AND PAIN AWAY.
DREAMING, DREAMING, DREAMING,
DREAMING TAKES ME HOME.

DREAMING TIME,
    (Echo) DREAMING TIME
IS A CAT DESIGN.
    (Echo) IS A CAT DESIGN.
MARKING TIME,
    (Echo) MARKING TIME,
'TILL **BELOVED'S** MINE.
    (Echo) OH! PLEASE BE MINE.
THREE STEPS, FIVE BACK,
THREE BY FIVE I ROAM.
THREE STEPS, FIVE BACK,
SOON, I'LL GO HOME. (*PURR*)

Blackout

Scene 7: DODGING THE BULLET

Lights up, SHELTER, dogs on one side, cats on the other.

PETER NAPOLEON
Well kid, I've dodged this bullet long enough.

PUPPY
I don't get it.

PETER NAPOLEON
They just took away Little Max.

PUPPY
They tell me I won't miss what I've never used.

PETER NAPOLEON
Yeah, they promise you a lot of stuff. I'm still waiting for that bone factory.

LUCKY-CAT
I'm going to miss it. I live for Father's Day. With 280,012 kittens, the gifts just keep on coming.

MOM-CAT
The kittens just don't write like they used to, not since they had their "tummy tucks." *(air quotes)* I sure miss those lovely Pee-mail Mother's Day messages.

KITTEN
I don't get it.

LUCKY
You will. Oh, you will.

KITTEN
Why do they all have nekkid tummies—or other things—when they come back?

MOM-CAT
Like I said, tummy tuck. Humans are weird.

LUCKY
You got any catnip on you? Maybe I won't care so much if I'm mellow.

PUPPY
So what does Little Max get out of this?

PETER NAPOLEON
Well it sure ain't bragging rights.

PUPPY
Is there anything else?

PETER NAPOLEON
A new home.

PUPPY
A new home?! *(awed, hopeful)*

PETER NAPOLEON
In my book, that's worth the trade. (*sigh*) Almost. Gonna miss those leg-hugging marathons.

PUPPY
I don't get it.

PETER NAPOLEON
You will. Well, maybe you won't. That stuffed toy was always real attractive.

MOM-CAT
(*to LUCKY*) I'm ready for a rest. Sure, kittens are cute but they've got no off switch. And this milk bar is closed.

LUCKY
Yeah, I noticed you are saggin' and draggin a bit lately. Maybe it is time for that tummy tuck.

MOM-CAT
Hiss!

KITTEN
I don't get it.

LUCKY
Oh look, it's my turn. Time for a nip and tuck. Maybe a little off the sides? (*exits*)

KITTEN
I still don't get it.

PUPPY
(*looks offstage*) They just finished Little Max.

PETER NAPOLEON
Well, I'm next.

PUPPY
I didn't catch your name.

PETER NAPOLEON
The name's Peter. Peter Napoleon.

MOM-CAT
So when you come out you'll be a little Pee—

PETER NAPOLEON
Don't say it. Just don't say it. *(sighs)* Please just don't say it.

MOM-CAT
Napoleon? *(looks him up and down, he poses big-dog attitude)* Yes, I can see it.

KITTEN & PUPPY
(to each other, both of them frustrated and clueless) I don't get it!

PETER NAPOLEON
See ya on the flip side. And what was your name?

PUPPY
Dinky—*(cuts off, realizes can rename him/herself)*. I mean, Stubby.

PETER NAPOLEON
It fits. Or it will. *(exits)*

MOM-CAT
(looks up) My turn already? *(to kitten, smoothing fur, straightening)* You be good. I'll be back soon. And no matter how funny I look or smell, I'll still be your mother, remember that! *(exits)*

>PUPPY and KITTEN checking each other out.

PUPPY
You smell funny.

KITTEN
Oh yeah? Well you look funny! Don't you wag your stubby ass-ets at me, I can take ya! *(postures like a boxer and hisses)*

PUPPY
What? Wagging? Oh sorry, when I get happy that happens.

KITTEN
Are you in for a tummy tuck, too? Funny, you don't look saggy.

PUPPY
No, I'm Stubby. I hear this is my ticket to a new home.

KITTEN
I'd like a forever home. But I really don't like dogs.

PUPPY
I really don't like cats.

KITTEN
What d'ya think the chances are we'll be adopted together?

PUPPY
You never can tell.

KITTEN
Is there anything we can share?

PUPPY
Warm bed and a loving heart. Deal? *(wags)*

KITTEN
Deal. *(purrs)*

Blackout.

Scene 8, IT'S TIME

The scene plays on a bare stage. No "animals" are seen. The stage is blue, and the only set pieces are a table, a catch-pole (pole with a rope attached) and a syringe. Alternatively, project the image on a screen—Video is available.

OLD GRUFF (VO1)
Who...who's gonna adopt a three-legged dog.

BASSET
What's that?

OLD GRUFF
I said, "Who's gonna adopt a three-legged dog?

MUTT
Knock it off. I'm trying to sleep.

YOUNG VOICE (VO2)
I don't even know how I got here. I was just walking along, and this man with a long pole put a rope around my neck, and here I am. Minding my own business, and—

BASSET
"Three legs" you say... Try going around with one eye. One eye and a chewed up ear.

MUTT
Now, THAT'LL sure make someone want to take you home with 'em.

YOUNG VOICE
What is this place? Are they going to help us?

MUTT
Oh, they're going to help you, OK. They're going to help you right into the--

OLD GRUFF
Shut up. Don't scare him.

MUTT
What are there, four of us left? There were seven or eight?

YOUNG VOICE
Seven or eight what?

BASSET
Never mind. Don't listen to them.

YOUNG VOICE
But I want to know--

BASSET
No you don't.

OLD GRUFF
Did you know that I spent most of my life outside? I was tied to a fence, and had a cardboard box to live in. Did you ever watch snow bleed through a cardboard box? Yeah...I've been tied to fences, trees, an old tire.

BASSET
Try having some drunk "teach you a lesson" because you barked too much.

OLD GRUFF
You know how I lost my leg?

YOUNG VOICE
An accident of some kind?

OLD GRUFF
Sure, kid...if being thrown out of a moving car is an accident.

YOUNG VOICE
You're scaring me.

BASSET
He's right. Let's just try to get some rest, if we can--

MUTT
Rest. In here? We'll all be resting before long.

YOUNG VOICE
When we get out of here, maybe we can all just roam around together. Maybe we can find some place where we can--

OLD GRUFF
Sure, kid. We'll all roam around together. We'll eat sirloin steak, and we'll live in a big house. We'll have someone nice to toss a ball for us to chase--

BASSET
And, we'll have a soft dog bed to sleep in, too. That'd be nice. And, how about a lot of soft dirt so we can dig holes and bury soup bones?

MUTT
And, how about a big old cat to chase? Not to catch him or hurt him, but just to chase once in a while.

YOUNG VOICE
That sounds good! And, someone to pet us a lot. And, scratch our ears, too. And, and maybe under our chins.

BASSET
Nah...the side of the face. No, even better! A big old tummy rub! Now, that's living at its best. Nothing's better than a tummy--

Sound of a door opens and then closes.

YOUNG VOICE
What was that?

MUTT
That was Old Gruff, son. It's his time.

YOUNG VOICE
Time for what?

BASSET
In about five minutes... Well, Old Gruff's gonna have all four of his legs, again. He's gonna be eating sirloin steaks, and he's gonna be digging holes, burying those soup bones...

MUTT
And, he'll be getting those tummy rubs, and having his face scratched. I can just see him chasing that old cat around real soon, now.

BASSET
You rest now, son... Before too long we're all gonna see Old Gruff, and what a time we'll have...what a time.

Scene 9: CUZ I'M A DAWG

Lights up on KITTEN and SWAGGER as BLUESY DAWG enters SHELTER area.

BLUESY DAWG
Didja see him? The skunk? Did he come this way, where did he go…

KITTEN
Look, who's that?

SWAGGER
More strays? The gift that keeps on giving.

BLUESY DAWG
Hey, I've been kicked out of swankier joints than this. And I've already been nipped in the bud, so no more baby gifts from this one, thank you very much! *(starts to leave.)*

SWAGGER
Sit. Stay. *(aside to KITTEN)* Always wanted to say that. Anyway, it's not like we can leave. What are you, anyway? *(puffs up)* I'm a purebred.

BLUESY DAWG
Purebred what?

SWAGGER
Purebred Chow Hound. (*others laugh*) What's so funny?

BLUESY DAWG
(to KITTEN) Are you something special or just a cat?

KITTEN
(hisses) There's no such thing as just a cat! *(to PUPPY)* See I told you I really don't like dogs.

> *Music* <u>CUZ I'M A DAWG</u> *begins, and next line spoken during introduction.*

BLUESY DAWG
(Sighs) You're not the only one. I got kicked outta the house, even though I did everything right! (*s/he sings*)

I'LL BE SNIFFIN' YOU.
YES, I'LL BE SNIFFIN' YOU.
TELL YA HOW IT GOES...
WISH I HAD BARBARA STREISAND'S NOSE.
CUZ I'LL BE SNIFFIN' YOU.

GONNA WET YO TREES [*alt lyric: GRASS*].
YEAH, GONNA WET YO TREES/*GRASS*.
IT BRINGS ME LOTSA JOY.
[*alt lyric: IT SETS MY TAIL A-WHIRL*]
CALL ME DA INCONTINENT BOY/*GIRL*.
I'M GONNA WET YO TREES/*GRASS*.

CUZ I'M A DAWG.
A JIP-JUMPIN' GROUND THUMPIN' DAWG.
I'LL MAKE A MESS OF YO LAWN.
SURE AS DA DAY YOU WAS BAWN.
CUZ I'M A DAWG.

GOT SPRAYED BY A SKUNK.
YEAH, GOT SPRAYED BY A SKUNK.
GET TOMATO JUICE BY DA JUG,
CUZ I'LL BE RUBBIN' DA SMELL ON YO RUG.
GOT SPRAYED BY A SKUNK.

GONNA HOWL ALL NIGHT.
YEP, GONNA HOWL ALL NIGHT.
IT'S GONNA IRRITATE YOU,
BUT, MAN IT'S WHAT I DO.
GONNA HOWL ALL NIGHT.

CUZ I'M A DAWG
A JIP-JUMPIN' GROUND THUMPIN' DAWG.
I'LL KNOCK OVER MY WATER BOWL,
WHEN I'M TOTALLY OUTTA CONTROL,
CUZ I'M A DAWG.

CUZ I'M A DAWG
A JIP-JUMPIN' GROUND THUMPIN' DAWG.
I'LL KNOCK OVER MY WATER BOWL,
WHEN I'M TOTALLY OUTTA CONTROL,
CUZ I'M A DAWG.

Blackout

Scene 10, PUFF PUFF

> *LIGHTS UP in SHELTER room, PUFF PUFF sleeping on floor, MOM approaches.*

PRACTICAL CAT
Puff Puff… Puff Puff. *(No response, she pokes him, finally yells.)* OH PUFF PUFF!

PUFF-PUFF
Will you lay off of that "Puff Puff" stuff.

PRACTICAL CAT
Oh, that's right…*(winks at other cats)* you're, what was it? Buck? George? Raymond? Maybe, Ralph? No, let's see…John Wayne?

PUFF-PUFF
I don't care what you call me. Just PLEASE, NOT PUFF-PUFF!

KITTEN
OK, Dino *(laughs)*.

PUFF-PUFF

"Dino"...Yeah, I like it!

PRACTICAL CAT

Anyway, Puff Puff...you were saying, now what got you out on the streets?

PUFF-PUFF

(*Sighs, not happy*) Well, I still don't get it. Oh, I had a home, but my person was a hard-case I just could not get trained. Sent lots of messages, but she ignored every Pee-Mail note I left. I guess it was about the third time...no, maybe it was the seventieth time that I pooped in the planter that I...

PRACTICAL CAT

You pooped in the planter?

PUFF-PUFF

Yeah, well, anyway...

KITTEN

Why did you do that?

PUFF-PUFF

The planter offered some privacy. And digging ops. You ever try to dig stinky concrete?

PRACTICAL CAT

Idiot!

PUFF-PUFF

What?

PRACTICAL CAT

I said, "IDIOT."

KITTEN

Yeah, I've got to agree. Should have hid it better. Or left it out in the open and blamed the dog. (*Laughs and waves at the group of dogs.*) Didn't you have a litter box?

PUFF-PUFF

I did, one teeny little box clear down in the far corner of the basement in the laundry room, under a counter.

KITTEN

Sounds like a trap.

PUFF-PUFF
Tell me about it! No way to scope out enemy approaches from a horrible dinky-dog. And my person kept forgetting to scoop. They don't make cat-size gas masks, and I couldn't hold my breath and be creative at the same time. I could barely turn around in that teeny toilet without my nether regions hanging out.

PRACTICAL CAT
I like one box for solids and another for liquids, ya know?

PUFF-PUFF
(Dreamily) That sounds like heaven, so to speak...

PRACTICAL CAT
As it were...

PUFF-PUFF
So I crossed my furry legs as long as I could before the planter seduced me. And just as I assumed the position, BAM! I got smacked with a shoe, and was out on my ear, and in mid-euphoria, too. I had to finish on the lawn! On the lawn!! Well, I don't hafta to tell you how humiliating THAT was.

PRACTICAL CAT
Oh, sing me another sad song.

KITTEN
Yeah, me, too. You had it made, Dino, or, should I say, "Dummo."

PUFF-PUFF
You two should talk! You had two boxes and still couldn't hit the mark!

PRACTICAL CAT
Three boxes. 1+1 rule, one box per cat, plus one. (*Defensively*) It wasn't our fault. S/HE kept guarding the box and wouldn't let me near the facilities. . .

KITTEN
Don't blame me. It was that *(spit)* dog. I really don't like dogs.

PUPPY
(*Hurt*) Hey, I thought we were friends.

HOUND DOG
Sure, blame it on the dog. The dog's always a good patsy.

PUFF-PUFF
For once you're right. (*to other cats*) The dog outsmarted two cats? Really? Talk about humiliating. You want to tell me how a goof-ball dog made you snub the facilities? (*laughing*)

PUPPY
(*whispering to HOUND DOG*) Maybe cats don't like dogs grazing, you know, from the litter box. Isn't that how you lost your home? (*looks at other DOGS*) And you talked about chewing, and digging, and barking--

NAPOLEON
Nothing wrong with chewing, digging and barking. At least we don't crap in the planter.

HOUND DOG
Yeah, and our tails never lie. Cats wag an invitation for a sniff, then BAM! we get nailed with concealed cat weapons.

PRACTICAL CAT
(*Offended*) Cats don't wag. If a nosy dog can't understand a warning tail thump, you deserve what you get!

KITTEN
Wait a minute!

PUPPY
Listen to us!

KITTEN
Stop pointing paws at each other. We all lost homes for the same reason.

PUPPY
We must have done something *really bad*. Wish I knew what I did.

NAPOLEON
(*hanging head*) For a while I thought my name was "bad dog."

PRACTICAL CAT
My person used to call me "Kitty-Stop-That."

> *Intro for* <u>NORMAL</u>, *with following lines spoken over the music.*

KITTEN
Some of you want a second chance. I want a first chance at a forever home so help a kitten out.

PUPPY
Yeah. Think back, what were you doing just before—you know—you got kicked to the curb?

(PUFF-PUFF)
GONNA MATCH THAT SCRATCH
MAKE MY MARK, MARK, MARK,
WHILE THEY SNATCH TO CATCH
ME IN THE DARK, DARK, DARK.
CAN'T STOP MY PAWS
FROM MAKING CLAWS
BAD KITTY,
THAT'S MEEEE-OW.

(HOUND)
GONNA START MY DIGGIN'
CUZ I BEEN FIGGERIN'
HOW TO DIG A HOLE
CUZ I BEEN TOLL
YA NEED TO DO IT
SO THE BONE'LL FIT IT
YEAH, DIGGIN.

(PRACTICAL-CAT)
GOTTA LEAP AND CLIMB
UP THE WALL WALL WALL
COUNTER TIME IS PRIME
TV'S A BALL, BALL, BALL
COUNTERTOP CRUISING
IS SO AMUSING,
BAD KITTY
THAT'S MEEEE-OW.

(NAPOLEON)
CHEWIN'S REAL DANG GOOD
MAKE IT CARPET. MAKE IT WOOD
CHEWIN' AM MY LIFE,
IT CAUSES LOTS OF STRIFE
CAN'T CONROL MY GNAWING,
NO MORE HEM AND HAWING,
YEAH, CHEWIN'.

(ALL—OR PUPPY/KITTEN CHORUS)
SHE'S NOR-MAL, HE'S NOR-MAL, MEANT TO BE,
OH, CAN'T YOU SEE, HOLY GEE, JUST HEAR MY PLEA,
PERFECTLY NOR-MAL, TO ME.

(ALL CATS or FEATURE SOLO)
GOTTA NIP AND BITE
BUNNY KICK, KICK, KICK,
LURK AT NIGHT, PLAY AND FIGHT,
THEN I LICK, LICK, LICK,
ANKLE BITING,
AIN'T REALLY FIGHTING.
BAD KITTY,
THAT'S MEEEE-OW.

(ALL DOGS or FEATURE SOLO)
BARKING AT FAT SQUIRRELLS
ROUND THE TREE IN A SWIRL
VOCAL CORDS GET TIGHT
IT JUST AIN'T RIGHT
CATCHING A SQUIRRELLY TWIT
IT WON'T STOP MY BARKING FIT.
YEAH, BARKIN'.

(CATS)
GOTTA PEE AND POOP
OVER HERE, HERE, HERE,
IN THE SOUP WHEN I WHOOPS
OUT OF FEAR FEAR, FEAR,
I WANT A SAFE SPOT
FOR MY KITTY POT,
BAD KITTY,
THAT'S MEEE-OW.

(DOGS)
*SHOW ME A LEG THAT'S BARE
OR TROUSERS, I DON'T CARE.
I'LL BOUNCE REAL FAST
GOTTA MAKE IT LAST
GRINDIN' AND BUMPIN'
CAN'T STOP LEG A-HUMPIN'.
YEAH, HUMPIN'.

(*DOG ALTERNATE VERSION #2)
SHOW ME A FENCE RIGHT THERE
AN OPEN WINDOW, I DON'T CARE
I'LL LEAP REAL FAST
GOTTA MAKE A DASH,
HEADS UP, NO SLUMPIN',
CAN'T STOP FENCE A-JUMPIN'
YEAH, JUMPIN'.

(ALL CHORUS)
SHE'S NOR-MAL, HE'S NOR-MAL, MEANT TO BE,
OH, CAN'T YOU SEE, HOLY GEE, JUST HEAR MY PLEA,
PERFECTLY NOR-MAL, TO ME.

(PETS RAP—DOG AND CAT take turns)

FOR PAWS THAT CLAW HERE'S THE STANDARD ENTREATY,
OFFER LEGAL OPS FOR THAT SCRATCH GRAFFITI.
COUCH AND CARPET WILL INSPIRE,
THE SCRATCHES KITTIES MOST ADMIRE.
GIVE HER LEGAL SCRATCHING…
OR MAYHEM SHE'LL BE HATCHING! HISS! HISS!

DIGGEDY DOGS HAVE LOTS OF REASONS
COOL SPOTS FOR HOT DOGS, A HOLE CAN BE PLEASIN',
BUILD YOUR PUP A SAND BOX WITHOUT A BARRIER,
THAT'LL BANISH ANGST FROM YOUR HOLY TERRIER.
CAN YOU DIG IT? CAN YOU DIG IT?

TOP CATS CLIMB, THAT'S A KITTY RULE
GOTTA PERCH AWAY FROM THAT DOGGY DROOL
COUNTER TOPS ARE PRIME FELINE TERRITORY,
CUZ HIGH RISE OPS ARE KITTY MANDATORY,
GIVE CATS HIGHER SECOND-STORY OPTIONS
FOR FELINES TO CLAIM BETTER LEAP-ADOPTIONS.
TOP CAT HERE! TOP CAT HERE!

WHAT'S UP WITH ALL THE CHEWIN'?
YOU SAY HE'S OVER DOIN'?
THE HOUSE, THE YARD EXPLORED?
SOUNDS LIKE HE'S MERELY BORED.
EASY FIX—GIVE 'EM MORE LICKS.
WITH CHEWS YOU CAN'T BE STINGY,
LET 'EM BINGY! BACON, BACON, BACON!

KITTEN ALL BITE-Y? WELL ALRIGHTY.
FLUFFY WITH CUTICITY THAT WILL BEWITCH,
BUT KITTENS GO-GO-GO AND GOT NO KITTY OFF-SWITCH.
ENJOY AND HANG ON TIGHT, THOUGH, CUZ EVERY KITTEN DUNCE
WILL OUTGROW THE FUN IN ONLY NINE MONTHS.

BARKING FILLS THE BORING DAY,
GIVE HIM SOMETHING BETTER TO SAY.
LIKE, FOR INSTANCE…LET'S PLAY!
FRISBEE, ANYONE? WANNA PLAY?

ONE BOX PER KITTY PLUS ONE I SAY,
MAKES MOST LITTER-ARY WOES GO CLEAN AWAY.
*HUMPIN' YOUR LEG GETS A LOT OF ATTENTION
(*Alt text: *JUMPIN' A FENCE GETS A LOT OF ATTENTION*)
AND DARE I MENTION, IT RELIEVES DOGGY TENSION.
WOOF, BABY!

(CAT AND DOG VERSES COMBINED)

GONNA MATCH THAT
SCRATCH
MAKE MY MARK, MARK,
MARK,
WHILE THEY SNATCH TO
CATCH
ME IN THE DARK, DARK, DARK.
CAN'T STOP MY PAWS
FROM MAKING CLAWS
BAD KITTY, THAT'S MEEEE-OW

GONNA START MY DIGGIN'
CUZ I BEEN FIGGERIN'
HOW TO DIG A HOLE
CUZ I BEEN TOLL
YA NEED TO DO IT
SO THE BONE'LL FIT IT
YEAH, DIGGIN.

GOTTA LEAP AND CLIMB
UP THE WALL WALL WALL
COUNTER TIME IS PRIME
TV'S A BALL, BALL, BALL
COUNTERTOP CRUISING
IS SO AMUSING,
BAD KITTY
THAT'S MEEEE-OW.

CHEWIN'S REAL DANG GOOD
MAKE IT CARPET. MAKE IT
WOOD
CHEWIN' AM MY LIFE
IT CAUSES LOTS OF STRIFE
CAN'T STOP MY GNAWING
NO MORE HEM AND HAWING
YEAH, CHEWIN'.

GOTTA NIP AND BITE
BUNNY KICK, KICK, KICK,
LURK AT NIGHT, PLAY AND
FIGHT,
THEN I LICK, LICK, LICK,
ANKLE BITING,
AIN'T REALLY FIGHTING.
BAD KITTY,
THAT'S MEEEE-OW.

BARKING AT FAT SQUIRRELS
ROUND THE TREE IN A SWIRL
VOCAL CORDS GET TIGHT
IT JUST AIN'T RIGHT
CATCHING A SQUIRRELLY
TWIT
IT WON'T STOP MY BARKING
FIT.
YEAH, BARKIN'.

GOTTA PEE AND POOP
OVER HERE, HERE, HERE,
IN THE SOUP WHEN I WHOOPS
OUT OF FEAR FEAR, FEAR,
I WANT A SAFE SPOT
FOR MY KITTY POT,
BAD, BAD KITTY,
THAT'S MEEE-OW.

SHOW ME A LEG THAT'S BARE
OR TROUSERS, I DON'T CARE.
I'LL BOUNCE REAL FAST
GOTTA MAKE IT LAST
GRINDIN' AND BUMPIN'
CAN'T STOP LEG HUMPIN'.
YEAH, HUMPIN'. **

(**DOG ALTERNATE VERSION)
SHOW ME A FENCE RIGHT THERE
AN OPEN WINDOW, I DON'T CARE
I'LL LEAP REAL FAST, GOTTA MAKE A DASH,
HEADS UP, NO SLUMPIN', CAN'T STOP FENCE A-JUMPIN'
YEAH, JUMPIN'.

(CHORUS)
SHE'S NOR-MAL, HE'S NOR-MAL, MEANT TO BE,
OH, CAN'T YOU SEE, HOLY GEE, JUST HEAR MY PLEA,
PERFECTLY NOR-MAL, TO ME.

      OFFSTAGE VOICE 1
(*Shouting*) That's it! You're outta here!
           Door slam. Blackout.

(INTERMISSION)

ACT 2

Scene 1, DOG ON THE RUN

> *OUTDOORS area. Spotlight on soloist center stage, as music for <u>DOG ON THE RUN</u> begins. MUTT sings.*

BORN AT NIGHT IN QUITE A FIX,
FIVE LITTLE PUPS, AND I MADE SIX.
SCRAPPIN' AND FIGHTIN' FROM NIGHT TIL SUN.
SUCH IS LIFE FOR A DOG ON THE RUN.

GROWED UP FAST, AND GROWED UP TOUGH.
NOT MUCH FOOD, NEVER HAD ENOUGH.
HIDIN' AND SCARED FROM NIGHT TIL SUN.
SUCH IS LIFE FOR A DOG ON THE RUN.

FOR A RUNNIN' DOG, LIFE AIN'T FUN.
AIN'T NO FUN FOR A DOG ON THE RUN.
PRAYIN' FOR A BETTER DAY,
MAKE THE BAD THINGS GO AWAY.

HAVE NO LIFE TO BRAG ABOUT.
HOW CAN YA BRAG WHEN YOU'RE LIVIN' OUT?
DON'T KNOW WHERE THE NEXT MEAL'S COMIN' FROM.
SUCH IS LIFE FOR A DOG ON THE RUN.

NEVER HAD NO HOME, BUT WISH I HAD.
ALL MY LIFE'S JUST BEEN ALL BAD.
WISH FOR A PLACE, SURE WANTED ONE.
SUCH IS LIFE FOR A DOG ON THE RUN.

FOR A RUNNIN' DOG, LIFE AIN'T NO FUN.
AIN'T NO FUN FOR A DOG ON THE RUN.
PRAYIN FOR A BETTER DAY,
MAKE THE BAD THINGS GO AWAY.

(sung up an octave if possible)
FOR A RUNNIN' DOG, LIFE AIN'T NO FUN.
AIN'T NO FUN FOR A DOG ON THE RUN.
PRAYIN FOR A BETTER DAY,
MAKE THE BAD THINGS GO AWAY.

I'M AN OLD DOG NOW, DON'T MOVE TOO GOOD.
CAN'T DODGE THE THINGS I KNOW I SHOULD.
LOOKIN' FOR A PLACE TO LAY MY HEAD.
WISHIN' FOR A NICE WARM BED.

LORD TAKE ME HOME, IF YOU MUST.
WON'T COMPLAIN. WON'T MAKE A FUSS.
HAD A HARD LIFE. SAW MY LAST SUN.
SUCH IS LIFE FOR A DOG ON THE RUN

FOR A RUNNIN' DOG, LIFE AIN'T NO FUN.
AIN'T NO FUN FOR A DOG ON THE RUN.
PRAYIN' FOR A BETTER DAY.
MAKE THE BAD THINGS GO AWAY.

(sung up an octave)
FOR A RUNNIN' DOG, LIFE AIN'T NO FUN.
AIN'T NO FUN FOR A DOG ON THE RUN.
PRAYIN' FOR A BETTER DAY.
MAKE THE BAD THINGS GO AWAY.

PRAYIN' FOR A BETTER DAY.
MAKE THE BAD THINGS GO AWAY.

Blackout.

Scene 2, SHOW DOG

> *ALLEY, area light up on monologue.*

SWAGGER-PUP

I live a wonderful life. I'm pampered, petted, and made a fuss over daily. I travel, and see new things. A lot of people look at me and compliment me. People want to touch me and hold me. I live around others like me who just can't get enough attention. I eat well and have just about everything in life that I want. I'm clipped, brushed, combed and blow-dried. Nothing is too good for me. My people are proud of me, and rightly so...I'm a show dog. I'm elite...one of a kind...the best of the best.

OFFSTAGE VOICE 2

Get a load of THAT guy. The perfect dog...the perfect specimen...a wonder to behold.

SWAGGER

Ya hear that? He's right. I am perfect. (*gives cheesy thumbs-up look.*) My coat shines like a newly waxed car. My ears point skyward as if God himself were calling me. My poses are a study in wonderissity...

OFFSTAGE VOICE 2

That's not a real word!

SWAGGER

It is now, for I can do no wrong. For I wish it to be so...for I AM...ta-daah...Prince Wilhelm Vonprickington Northtarryington Johntarthy Fullbright.

OFFSTAGE VOICE 2

Oh, yeah...well, what do they call you when you're not busy being perfect?

SWAGGER

Dwayne. But, that's only for my few selected friends. Anyway, I thought I'd show you just how it's done, how to pile up the ribbons, how I became me.

This is how to point *(demonstrates)*. How to heel *(places hands out like a faith-healer)*. I don't have that one perfected. Yet. How to roll over *(rolls over and strikes a pose)*. How to stroll the winner's circle *(struts around)*. How to be camera ready *(does several over the top faces)*.

Yep, it's not easy being me. So many expectations. And, those other dogs! I mean is it just me, or do all wiener dogs smell funny? Don't all Chihuahuas shake? Doesn't every Bloodhound have a face like a melted Eskimo pie? And German Shepherds...all I can say is, "Go find a fire hydrant, Fritz! I'm not impressed."

Oh, I know, you resent me because of what I am. Sure, I'm handsome *(cheesy thumbs up look again).* I'm shiny. I eat like a king. I'm alert. I'm pampered. I'm every dog's dream of perfection, but can I help it? I am...A SHOW DOG. Look upon the perfection of me, and dream...dream and envy...dream and wish.

OFFSTAGE VOICE 2
Hey Dwayne! I just found half a pizza in the trash!

SWAGGER
(becoming very mutt-like and talking in a goofy voice) Hot dang! Trash food! One of my...*(aware of who he is)* Oh...I don't know. Who am I, of all dogs, to chase garbage can pizza? I'll look. I mean, what does it hurt to at least check it out? *(walks slowly, nonchalant, to the garbage cans and begins checking them out).*

OFFSTAGE VOICE 2
Wait a minute, Mr. Show Dog, why are you here? How'd Mr. Perfect lose his home?

SWAGGER
(hesitates) Not sure. But they kicked me out of a whole city, said my kind wasn't welcome. I think it had something to do with a new musical group came to our town. Ever heard of 'em? The Breed Band? *(dives into garbage can again, comes up with pizza and dashes offstage)*

Scene 3, INNAPPROPRIATE PET GIFTS

> *Two DOGS enter ALLEY as SWAGGER leaves.*

PUPPY
What's the worst gift you ever got?

PETER NAPOLEON
You ever get one of those pink and gray rubber bones? A million laughs on that.

PUPPY
I got one of those one time. There was this five-year-old kid in the neighborhood who kept tossing it at me, wanting me to catch it. Dang thing was like a missile. I didn't know how to catch, and I got beaned about 12 times before the kid finally got tired of throwing.

PETER NAPOLEON
See this? (*no teeth and lisping*) One of those things took out the tooth and split my lip.

PUPPY
Right there in the center, yeah, I can see it!

PETER NAPOLEON
No, here, here.

PUPPY
Where, mop-face, there's too much hair to see?

PETER NAPOLEON
Tell me about it. What about you, what's the worst gift you ever got?

PUPPY
A hotdog costume for Halloween. Oh, the shame of it all!

PETER NAPOLEON
I hear ya there, Oscar Meyer. If you're going to dress me up, I want to be a police dog—maybe get some respect. So…what's the best gift you ever got?

PUPPY
The guy I was with had just one leg. Every time he got a new pair of shoes, he gave me the other one. I hate that new shoe smell, though. That's how I got kicked out…chewed the wrong one, the one he wore. (*he sighs*) It smelled like him…heaven. So what's the best gift you ever got?

PETER NAPOLEON
(*long pause*) A home.

Lights fade to black.

Scene 4: BORROWED TIME

> *Spotlight on soloist in OUTDOOR area as music introduction plays of <u>EIGHT LIVES IN HEAVEN</u>. LUCKY CAT sings, with two treble background voices.*

I WAS GIVEN NINE LIVES,
BUT I FRITTERED AWAY ABOUT EIGHT.
BEEN BINGED, BONGED, BANGED AND TOSSED AROUND,
NEXT STOPS THAT OL' PEARLY GATE.

> *Spoken earnestly over background music.*

FIRST LIFE DONE WENT AWAY,
I'M LUCKY TO BE ALIVE.
THOUGHT IT WAS AN EASY SIX FOOT JUMP,
WHO KNEW I COULD ONLY JUMP FIVE?

SECOND LIFE, I WAS STOOPID.
I WAS COUNTIN' ON A LITTLE LUCK.
THOUGHT I'D IMPRESS MISS KITTY LE PURR,
BY DODGIN' A CEMENT TRUCK.

THIRD LIFE…NOT MY FAULT.
I WAS SLEEPIN' ON A SECOND FLOOR LEDGE.
WHAT SCHMUCK DOESN'T KNOW,
TO PUT RAILS ON THE BALCONY EDGE?

> *(Singing)*

FOURTH AND FIFTH I DON'T TALK ABOUT,
YOU CAN ASK ME ALL DAY LONG.
BUT WHEN A CAT TAKES ON A PACK OF DOGS,
IT JUST TURNS OUT WRONG.

> *(Spoken)*

SIXTH LIFE, I DON'T REMEMBER.
JUST CAIN'T RECALL THE DAY,
THAT I WAS CHASIN' THAT OL' FLYIN' SQUIRREL,
RIGHT ONTO THE MAIN HIGHWAY.

SEVENTH LIFE, JUST VANISHED
FASTER THAN YOU CAN SAY "POOF."
I WAS PRACTICIN' MY BALANCE ACT
ON THAT DANG TWO STORY ROOF.

NUMBER EIGHT, NOW THAT'S THE ONE
THAT MADE ME CHANGE MY WAYS.
GOT SMACKED BY A HARLEY, AND LAYIN' IN THE BARLEY,
MADE ME COUNT THE DAYS...

(Singing)

CUZ I WAS GIVEN NINE LIVES,
NOW, YA KNOW WHAT HAPPENED TO EIGHT.
YES, I WAS SMACKED, CRACKED, WHACKED AND TOSSED AROUND,
NEXT STOP'S THAT OL' PEARLY GATE...
ON THAT-UN, I THINK I'LL WAIT...
SEEIN' THAT PEARLY GATE.

Lights fade to blackout.

Scene 5, OLD DOGS TALKING.

Area lights up in ALLEY.

DOBERMAN
I used to glide through the air like a fighter jet. Yep, I'd get in position and—

CHIHUAHUA
(very nervous) And, then what?

DOBERMAN
Then I'd snarl and bark and slobber and...

BASSET
(cupping his ear to hear) Now, wait a minute. No one, and I mean NO ONE can slobber like I can. I practically invented slobbering.

CHIHUAHUA
You can't out slobber a bulldog.

BASSET
What? What's that? My hearing's not what it was, and...

CHIHUAHUA
(shouting) I said that you can't out slobber a bulldog.

BASSET
Why would I want to clobber a bullfrog?

DOBERMAN
(shouting) BULLDOG! He said, "BULLDOG!"

BASSET
Bullfrog. That's right. I used to catch bullfrogs. They'd wet in my mouth and I'd slobber, and...

CHIHUAHUA
(to all) Let it go. Hey, did you see that new Poodle? Just moved into the house down the street. Mamachiwawa...makes me wish I was a few years younger.

BASSET
Who's got a hunger?

DOBERMAN
He said HUN...why do I bother?

BASSET
Are we still talking about bullfrogs?

CHIHUAHUA
Hey, here she comes! Get your noses ready boys. It's sniffing time.

GLAMOUR
Well, hello boys. (*boy dogs start panting, sniffing, etc.*) I'd like to get to know each and every one of you sometime, but (*she winks*) on my terms.

BASSET
(*to all*) What's that? She's got worms? What'd she say?

DOBERMAN
WORMS! She said that she had...wait a minute. Now, you've got me doing it. "Terms." She said that she had terms.

BASSET
Oh, yeah. Worms. I had 'em once. Drug my butt along the carpet for weeks.

GLAMOUR
Is he OK?

DOBERMAN
He's fine. Just a little deaf.

CHIHUAHUA
How about dinner, my little chili pepper?

GLAMOUR
Can't now. Got a date down the street to meet a Bulldog.

BASSET
Gonna eat a bullfrog? Those things'll make you slobber.

GLAMOUR
(*sexy voice, looking at Basset*) OK...well...(*blows them a kiss*) See you later, boys. (*swishes off stage. They all watch her leave*)

DOBERMAN
That's someone I'm gonna get to know real soon!

CHIHUAHUA
Muy bueno! She's hotter than summer pavement!

BASSET
Why the heck would she want to eat a bullfrog? I did that once. Made me slobber real bad. (*to Doberman*) You were saying something about how you'd glide like a jet, or hated to get wet, or...what were we saying about bullfrogs? Oh, yeah...those things'll make you slobber.

Lights fade to black.

Scene 6, FURRY GIFTS

Black stage

OFFSTAGE VOICE 2

I thank You for allowing me to see in such vivid colors. A scratch beneath the chin, or a tummy rub are the colors of happiness. A catnip toy...maybe a thrown Frisbee, or a kind smile from a beloved human are the colors of joy. A full bowl of food is the color of satisfaction, and a warm place to sleep is the color of peace. Now, if I may, I want to ask that all dogs and cats everywhere might someday see in vivid colors, too. And please let the humans we love—especially the clueless ones—recognize our furry gifts to them. And might that day come soon. Amen

Lights slowly come up in SHELTER as music introduction of <u>THE MUSE</u> *begins. GOSPEL CAT enters and sings, and other singers (small ensemble, think gospel sound) enter one by one as their voice is added to the full chorus. A slide show coordinated to lyrics illustrates the many ways pets inspire owners as furry muses.*

PURRS INSPIRE, CLAWS SPARK A FIRE.
ICY NOSE AND WARM, WET KISS.
LONELY HOWL THAT'S ON THE PROWL,
SILK-SOFT FUR AND ANGRY HISS.

I DIDN'T CHOOSE THIS EASY TASK,
I WON'T REFUSE, NO NEED TO ASK.
NOTHING TO LOSE, THIS GIFT WILL LAST
FOR EVERMORE, I AM YOUR MUSE.

PAINTING PICTURES, SINGING RHYME,
WRITING MIXTURES, TALKING TIME.
INSPIRATION, YOURS AND MINE,
IT WAS MEANT TO BE.

BARKS ALERT, PAWS KICK UP DIRT.
SNUGGLE PARTNER LAPS TO SHARE.
EYEBLINK KISSES, NINE LIVES WISHES,
SHEDDING FUR FOR ALL TO WEAR.

I DIDN'T CHOOSE THIS EASY TASK,
I WON'T REFUSE, NO NEED TO ASK.
NOTHING TO LOSE, THIS GIFT WILL LAST
FOR EVERMORE, I AM YOUR MUSE.

ARTIST DREAMING COMES ALIVE,
HOPE REDEEMING AS THEY STRIVE,
SO THAT ALL OUR LOVE SURVIVES,
TRUST, AND YOU WILL SEE!

PAWS THAT DANCE A CATNIP TRANCE.
RUNNING BUDDIES, PILLOW SHARE.
WHISKER TICKLES, PLAYTIME GIGGLES,
WIGGLE BUMS AND DOORWAY DARE.

I DIDN'T CHOOSE THIS EASY TASK,
I WON'T REFUSE, NO NEED TO ASK.
NOTHING TO LOSE, THIS GIFT WILL LAST
FOR EVERMORE, I AM YOUR MUSE.

FEED YOUR PASSION BY DESIGN,
HEED THE VISION IN YOUR MIND.
'TIS YOUR DECISION, DON'T DECLINE
THIS PRECIOUS GIFT FROM ME.

I DIDN'T CHOOSE THIS EASY TASK,
I WON'T REFUSE, NO NEED TO ASK.
NOTHING TO LOSE, THIS GIFT WILL LAST
FOR EVERMORE, I AM YOUR MUSE.
FOR EVERMORE, I AM YOUR MUSE.

Scene 7, TV'D

All remain on stage in SHELTER, sleeping, playing, grooming, etc and eavesdropping on the following conversation.

PUPPY

What does it mean...TV'd?

KITTEN

What?

PUPPY
TV'd. What does that mean? Is it medicine, or something? I already got neutered, not a lot of fun. See, all I heard the people say one of us was going on TV. That's being TV'd, right?

KITTEN
(sighing) No! Gosh, you're clueless. Don't you remember last week. Spike and Mittens got all cleaned up and were gone for an hour, and a little while after they got back—

PUPPY
That's right. People came for them. They made faces, and they laughed and hugged them both. They made some kind of agreement, but Spike and Mittens never came back. They looked happy, though.

KITTEN
Spike and Mittens? Well, they were TV'd.

PUPPY
Spike was on his last hour, whatever that means. And, Mittens...well she looked like she was really ready to get outta here.

KITTEN
She was beautiful, wasn't she? That's what I want to look like. Her head was held high, her coat glistened, and her eyes were so clear. You could hear her purr from clear across the room.

PUPPY
Well, ol' Spike looked pretty good, himself. Soft coat... trimmed claws... tail wagging. Ya know...I never saw his tail wag. The whole time he was in here, I never saw his tail wag. Not until that day. He wagged so hard that he actually fell over. Now, THAT'S a happy pooch! I hope I have a reason to wag that hard.

KITTEN
With that stub of a tail, you're gonna hafta really work at it. (*PUPPY looks dejected*) But, I'll just bet you can do it. In fact, I know you can do it.

PUPPY
(looking much happier) Thanks, but I'm gonna wait until I have a reason. You know, I don't want to give it all away, now.

KITTEN
I understand.

PUPPY
Don't take this the wrong way. I don't usually compliment cats, but you look and smell nice. Really nice.

KITTEN
Really?

PUPPY
I'm just saying....

KITTEN
That's because I'm being TV'd today.

PUPPY
Then, why am I here?

KITTEN
I think you're being TV'd, too.

PUPPY
I still don't get it.

KITTEN
I heard the people say something about they take some of us to be on TV, whatever that is, then maybe...MAYBE we get homes.

PUPPY
REALLY! A HOME! You mean like Spike and Mittens? People will smile at us, and laugh and hug us?

KITTEN
Yes. That's what I think.

PUPPY
I'm in. I'm in for the short-haul, the long haul...haul me all over the place. I'm in! What's next? Tell me.

KITTEN
Oh, a bath, a blow dry, a nail trim...let's see...perfume, maybe...

PUPPY
Perfume? Heck, I'd let them rub me with road tar if it would get me a home.

OFFSTAGE VOICE 1
Ok, we're ready for the puppy, now. The TV people will be here soon, for the Gotcha Day promotion.

KITTEN
Good luck.

PUPPY
Thank you. You too. And, listen...you really do look and smell really nice. Oh...and do you think the rest of the dogs and cats might get TV'd?

KITTEN
I hope so. If we're really cute, maybe even more people will come here visit the rest of the dogs and cats. Wouldn't that be paw-some? When you really think about it, there's a lot of love that's represented here. A lot of love...

PUPPY
OK. I'm ready. Bring on the bath, the nail trim...even the perfume! Cuz I don't want to stay, I want to go home today. A home where I'm loved.

KITTEN
Me, too...a home where I'm loved.

KITTEN begins <u>GOTCHA DAY</u> song with first verse solo, slow and plaintiff, PUPPY joins, and slowly other CATS and DOGS draw near listening, more and more excited about being adopted. More voices SOLO or ENSEMBLE added with each verse, excitement building as tempo increases to a FULL CHORUS joyous, celebratory march.

(KITTEN)
GOTTA PRACTICE MY CUTE,
GONNA MAKE MY PLAY.
IT'S ABSOLUTE THAT
I DON'T WANNA STAY.
YES, I'M RESOLUTE,
LISTEN WHAT I SAY.
BARK IT PROUD AND STRONG,
PURR IT LOUD AND LONG,
IT'S GONNA BE MY, MY GOTCHA DAY.

(PUPPY)
CAT TAILS UP, FUR SLICKED DOWN,
USE YOUR FELINE PURRSONALITY.

(KITTEN)
DOG PAWS UP, HOWL THE SOUND.
GIVE THEM A DOGGY GUARANTEE!
BARK IT PROUD AND STRONG,

(PUPPY)
PURR IT LOUD AND LONG,

(BOTH)
THEY'RE GONNA LOVE ME, WAIT AND SEE.

(PUPPY)
GOTTA PRACTICE MY CUTE,
GONNA MAKE MY PLAY.
IT'S ABSOLUTE THAT
I DON'T WANNA STAY.
YES, I'M RESOLUTE,
LISTEN WHAT I SAY.

(KITTEN)
BARK IT PROUD AND STRONG,

(PUPPY)
PURR IT LOUD AND LONG,

(BOTH)
IT'S GONNA BE MY, MY GOTCHA DAY.

(ASSIGN VARIOUS GROUPS/SOLOS)

PAW THE AIR, TAP THAT ARM,
SHOW YOUR SPECIAL KITTY
CAT DEXTERITY.
TUMMIES BARE SHOW NO HARM.
DOGGY GRINS REVEAL SINCERITY.
BARK IT PROUD AND STRONG,
PURR IT LOUD AND LONG,
THEY'RE GONNA LOVE ME, WAIT AND SEE.

GOTTA PRACTICE MY CUTE,
GONNA MAKE MY PLAY.
IT'S ABSOLUTE THAT
I DON'T WANNA STAY.
YES, I'M RESOLUTE,
LISTEN WHAT I SAY.
BARK IT PROUD AND STRONG,
PURR IT LOUD AND LONG,
IT'S GONNA BE MY, MY GOTCHA DAY.

TIP-TOE DANCE, POUNCE AND FLY,
CELEBRATE YOUR EXPERT
KITTY CAT BALLET.
PUPPY PRANCE, DON'T BE SHY.
DEMONSTRATE LAP SNUGGLES
RIGHT AWAY.
BARK IT PROUD AND STRONG,
PURR IT LOUD AND LONG,
THEY'RE GONNA LOVE ME, WAIT AND SEE.

(ALL)
GOTTA PRACTICE MY CUTE,
GONNA MAKE MY PLAY.
IT'S ABSOLUTE THAT
I DON'T WANNA STAY.
YES, I'M RESOLUTE,
LISTEN WHAT I SAY.
BARK IT PROUD AND STRONG,
PURR IT LOUD AND LONG,
IT'S GONNA BE MY, MY GOTCHA DAY.

Choreographed march formations continue, becoming faster and more joyous and hopeful, with stylized "dog" or "cat" specific behaviors incorporated (scratching, paws up, wagging, playing with toys, showing tummies, grooming each other, etc). Design the stage movement for the following counterpoint melodies to be mirrored in the actors' actions/choreography. OWNERS enter shelter toward end of song, observing cat and dogs and making note of which to adopt.

STRAYS, the MUSICAL

CAT TAILS UP, FUR SLICKED DOWN,
USE YOUR FELINE PURRSONALITY.
DOG PAWS UP, HOWL THE SOUND.
GIVE THEM A DOGGY GUARANTEE!
BARK IT PROUD AND STRONG,
PURR IT LOUD AND LONG,
THEY'RE GONNA LOVE ME,
WAIT AND SEE.

PAW THE AIR, TAP THAT ARM,
SHOW YOUR SPECIAL KITTY
CAT DEXTERITY.
TUMMIES BARE SHOW NO HARM.
DOGGY GRINS REVEAL SINCERITY.
BARK IT PROUD AND STRONG,
PURR IT LOUD AND LONG,
THEY'RE GONNA LOVE ME,
WAIT AND SEE.

TIP-TOE DANCE, POUNCE AND FLY,
CELEBRATE YOUR EXPERT
KITTY CAT BALLET.
PUPPY PRANCE, DON'T BE SHY.
DEMONSTRATE LAP SNUGGLES
RIGHT AWAY.
BARK IT PROUD AND STRONG,
PURR IT LOUD AND LONG,
THEY'RE GONNA LOVE ME,
WAIT AND SEE.

GOTTA PRACTICE MY CUTE,
GONNA MAKE MY PLAY.
IT'S ABSOLUTE THAT
I DON'T WANNA STAY.
YES, I'M RESOLUTE,
LISTEN WHAT I SAY.
BARK IT PROUD AND STRONG,
PURR IT LOUD AND LONG,
IT'S GONNA BE MY
MY GOTCHA DAY.

GOTTA PRACTICE MY CUTE,
GONNA MAKE MY PLAY.
IT'S ABSOLUTE THAT
I DON'T WANNA STAY.
YES, I'M RESOLUTE,
LISTEN WHAT I SAY.
BARK IT PROUD AND STRONG,
PURR IT LOUD AND LONG,
IT'S GONNA BE MY, MY GOTCHA DAY.

GOTTA PRACTICE MY CUTE,
GONNA MAKE MY PLAY.
IT'S ABSOLUTE THAT
I DON'T WANNA STAY.
YES, I'M RESOLUTE,
LISTEN WHAT I SAY.
BARK IT PROUD AND STRONG,
PURR IT LOUD AND LONG,
IT'S GONNA BE MY, MY GOTCHA DAY.

GOTTA PRACTICE MY CUTE,
GONNA MAKE MY PLAY.
IT'S ABSOLUTE THAT
I DON'T WANNA STAY.
YES, I'M RESOLUTE,
LISTEN WHAT I SAY.
BARK IT PROUD AND STRONG,
PURR IT LOUD AND LONG,
IT'S GONNA BE MY, MY GOTCHA DAY.

Scene 8, NOBODY'S DOG/CAT

>*SPOTLIGHT on OWNERS as they speak, indicating the pets.*

OWNER 1

Today I found Nobody's Dog. Her ribs were beginning to show through a once shiny black coat. At first, she tucked her tail tightly and ran, then, ever hopeful, returned with a tentative wag.

OWNER 2

I bet she was cute as a baby. Somebody picked her out special, took her home, and made her believe she would always be loved; but some humans change their minds and their loves as often as dirty socks. Even so, the betrayed black dog is still loving them, futilely waiting for them to come back for her. She had a name once, and now she can't understand, for you see, a pet's love never dies.

OWNER 1

Today, I found Nobody's Cat, one of millions abandoned each year by owners that take the coward's way out. They won't see her slowly starve or freeze to death, be hit by a car, or live at the mercy of strangers as she begs for a scrap of attention.

OWNER 1 & 2

Today, I rescued Nobody's Dog (Cat).

OWNER 2

Finally, she'll be fed, she'll be loved, and maybe she'll be claimed by a more fitting, deserving human into a home where pets are always loved and are never thrown away on a cruel whim. But there are always more cats and dogs, and each still yearns to be ….

OWNER 1 & 2

Somebody's Dog (Cat) once more.

>*Blackout*

Scene 9: PERFECT

Cage bars moved into position during blackout. AREA LIGHT UP on NOBODY'S CAT/DOG who deliver lines from behind bars. Rest of cats, dogs, puppies and kittens in dim light, positioned around stage, poised to "practice their cute" as prospective adopters arrive.

NOBODY'S DOG

Who...who's gonna adopt a three-legged dog?

NOBODY'S CAT

"Three legs" you say... Try going around with one eye. One eye and a chewed up ear. No amount of practicing my cute is going to help.

NOBODY'S DOG

Right, they want cute, and who can blame 'em? Look at the puppies and kittens, they're so hopeful, so excited, they have their whole life ahead of them.

NOBODY'S CAT

They're perfect.

NOBODY'S DOG

Why are we even here? Nobody will see us--

NOBODY'S CAT

Well, Somebody found me, and Somebody found you and now we're safe. That's more than I've had in a long time. And I heard my rescuer say, "Even the least of these deserves a chance—"

NOBODY'S DOG

What does that mean?

NOBODY'S CAT

I don't know. But I hope maybe we'll find out today.

Music begins LEAST OF THESE
NOBODY'S DOG begins with solo.

I WAS COLD, YET YOU WARMED MY HEART.
I WAS HURT, AND YOU HEALED MY PAIN.
I WAS AFRAID AND LOST,
YOU CAN'T KNOW THE COST
TO GAMBLE THAT THIS CHANCE
WON'T BE IN VAIN.

THE LEAST OF THESE,
THE LEAST OF THESE,
I WANT TO BE THE LEAST OF THESE.
WHEN YOU LOOK AT ME,
WONDER WHAT YOU SEE
OH PLEASE CHOOSE ME,
THE LEAST OF THESE.

(Either ONE or TWO "owner" soloists, observes "cute" posing pets seeking to be adopted, obviously tempted but holding back...)

JUST LOOKING, TO PASS THE TIME
NOT READY. I HIDE MY PAIN.
MISSING HIM. BUT I DO FINE.
CAN'T RISK MY HEART IN VAIN,
IT'S SAFER TO ABSTAIN,
WON'T EVER, WON'T EVER
FIND SUCH LOVE AGAIN.
HE WAS PER-FECT,
CAN'T YOU SEE,
PERFECT IN EVERY WAY.

(OWNER #2 enters, following DIALOGUE spoken over top of PERFECT chorus. FULL CHORUS or PUPPY-KITTEN DUET softly under dialogue)

PER-FECT, PER-FECT
COME WHAT MAY,
HE WAS OKAY EVERYDAY
IN EVERY WAY
NORMALLY PERFECT I SAY.

STRAYS, the MUSICAL

OWNER 1
SHE spit up hairballs in my husband's shoes—Ex-husband now.

OWNER 2
HE was a constant pest with that stupid tennis ball.

OWNER 1
Just found a catnip mouse…in the silverware drawer.

OWNER 2
It's been six months but there's still fur everywhere.

OWNER 1 & 2 TOGETHER
The place is so empty now.

> *NOBODY'S CAT sings next solo, as OWNERS continue to interact with PETS as they beg for adoption.*

I WAS HUNGRY, AND YOU GAVE ME FOOD.
I WAS THIRSTY, AND YOU GAVE ME DRINK.
AND I WAS JUST A STRAY,
AND YOU LET ME STAY,
BROUGHT ME INTO YOUR LIFE,
BACK FROM THE BRINK.

(NOBODY'S DOG & CAT)	(add OWNERS duet)
THE LEAST OF THESE,	PER-FECT, PER-FECT
THE LEAST OF THESE	COME WHAT MAY,
I WANT TO BE THE	HE WAS OKAY
LEAST OF THESE.	EVERYDAY
WHEN YOU LOOK AT ME,	IN EVERY WAY
WONDER WHAT YOU SEE	NORMALLY PERFECT I SAY.
OH PLEASE CHOOSE ME,	
THE LEAST OF THESE.	

> *OWNER sings, has an "aha" moment, finds the one perfect pet (blind, with three legs, puppy/kitten or old, you choose) that is THE perfect choice!*

JUST LOOKING, TO PASS THE TIME
I'M READY TO HONOR THE PAIN.
MISSING HIM. BUT I'LL DO FINE.
MUST RISK MY HEART AGAIN,
NO LONGER CAN REFRAIN.
NEVER KNEW, NEVER KNEW
I'D FIND SUCH LOVE AGAIN,
BUT YOU'RE PER-FECT, NOW I SEE,
PERFECT IN EVERY WAY.

Depending on cast numbers, additional OWNERS may enter, interact with pets and choose one or more (NOBODY'S DOG/CAT or others) to adopt but ignore PARIAH CAT as she silently entreats, going from owner to owner.

(MALE CATS & DOGS)
I WAS HUNGRY,
AND YOU GAVE ME FOOD.
I WAS THIRSTY, AND YOU GAVE ME DRINK.
AND I WAS JUST A STRAY,
AND YOU LET ME STAY,
BROUGHT ME INTO YOUR LIFE,
BACK FROM THE BRINK.

(OWNERS)
JUST LOOKING, TO PASS THE TIME
I'M READY TO HONOR THE PAIN.
MISSING HIM. BUT I'LL DO FINE.
MUST RISK MY HEART AGAIN,
NO LONGER CAN REFRAIN

(MALE VOICES)
THE LEAST OF THESE,
THE LEAST OF THESE,
I WANT TO BE THE LEAST OF THESE.
WHEN YOU LOOK AT ME,
WONDER WHAT YOU SEE
OH PLEASE CHOOSE ME,
THE LEAST OF THESE.

(TREBLE VOICES)
PER-FECT, PER-FECT
COME WHAT MAY,
HE WAS OKAY EVERYDAY
IN EVERY WAY
NORMALLY PERFECT
I SAY.

(OWNERS)
NEVER KNEW, NEVER KNEW
I'D FIND SUCH LOVE AGAIN,
BUT YOU'RE PER-FECT, NOW I SEE,
PERFECT IN EVERY WAY.

(MALE VOICES)	(TREBLE VOICES)	(OWNERS)
THE LEAST OF THESE,	PER-FECT, PER-FECT	NEVER KNEW, NEVER KNEW
THE LEAST OF THESE,	COME WHAT MAY,	I'D FIND SUCH LOVE AGAIN,
I WANT TO BE THE LEAST OF THESE.	HE WAS OKAY EVERYDAY IN EVERY WAY	BUT YOU'RE PER-FECT, NOW I SEE,
WHEN YOU LOOK AT ME, WONDER WHAT YOU SEE, OH PLEASE CHOOSE ME, THE LEAST OF THESE.	NORMALLY PERFECT I SAY.	PERFECT IN EVERY WAY.

PARIAH CAT not chosen stands by herself when a late-arriving OWNER sees, beckons, and she runs with joy into HIS/HER arms.

Scene 10: PICK OF THE LITTER

Dialogue under music intro of <u>RAINBOW PETS.</u>

OWNER 3
(to audience) Big ones, small ones, purebreds, mutts, babies to old fogies. Stray today, gone home tomorrow? That's what I'm talking about! We got your pick of the litter right here. Doesn't matter how they got here. What matters is what happens next. . . After all they're exactly the same--only different. And that's a beautiful thing!

(*PARIAH CAT solo*)
BLACK AND WHITE, BRINDLE OR TABBY,
MERLE OR BROWN, SABLE, ABBY,
PERSIAN, COLLIE, WHOLE OR FIXED,
RAINBOW PETS A PERFECT MIX.

(*TRIO TREBLE VOICES JOIN PARIAH CAT*)

BLACK AND WHITE, BRINDLE OR TABBY, MERLE OR BROWN, SABLE, ABBY, PERSIAN, COLLIE, WHOLE OR FIXED, RAINBOW PETS A PERFECT MIX.	BLACK AND WHITE, BRINDLE OR TABBY, MERLE OR BROWN, SABLE, ABBY, PERSIAN, COLLIE, WHOLE OR FIXED, RAINBOW PETS A PERFECT MIX.	BLACK AND WHITE, BRINDLE OR TABBY, MERLE OR BROWN, SABLE, ABBY, PERSIAN, COLLIE, WHOLE OR FIXED, RAINBOW PETS A PERFECT MIX.

BLACK AND WHITE,	BLACK AND WHITE,	BLACK AND WHITE,
BRINDLE OR TABBY,	BRINDLE OR TABBY,	BRINDLE OR TABBY,
MERLE OR BROWN,	MERLE OR BROWN,	MERLE OR BROWN,
SABLE, ABBY,	SABLE, ABBY,	SABLE, ABBY,
PERSIAN, COLLIE,	PERSIAN, COLLIE,	PERSIAN, COLLIE,
WHOLE OR FIXED,	WHOLE OR FIXED,	WHOLE OR FIXED,
RAINBOW PETS A	RAINBOW PETS A	RAINBOW PETS A
PERFECT MIX.	PERFECT MIX.	PERFECT MIX.

(*ALL CHORUS*)
I WAS YOUNG, I WAS OLD.
I WAS RESCUED, I WAS SOLD.
I WAS SICK, AND YOU WERE KIND.
BY SOME MYSTIC MASTER'S DESIGN
CAN'T YOU SEE, MEANT TO BE,
YOU WILL ALWAYS BE MINE.

WHOOPS OR	WHOOPS OR	WHOOPS OR
PLANNED, SHOWN OR	PLANNED, SHOWN OR	PLANNED, SHOWN OR
BANNED,	BANNED,	BANNED,
SHELTER, RESCUE,	SHELTER, RESCUE,	SHELTER, RESCUE,
FOSTER, POUND,	FOSTER, POUND,	FOSTER, POUND,
BOTTLE BABIES,	BOTTLE BABIES,	BOTTLE BABIES,
PUREBRED LADIES,	PUREBRED LADIES,	PUREBRED LADIES,
PERFECT, DAMAGED,	PERFECT, DAMAGED,	PERFECT, DAMAGED,
ALL ARE FOUND.	ALL ARE FOUND.	ALL ARE FOUND.

WHOOPS OR	WHOOPS OR	WHOOPS OR
PLANNED, SHOWN OR	PLANNED, SHOWN OR	PLANNED, SHOWN OR
BANNED,	BANNED,	BANNED,
SHELTER, RESCUE,	SHELTER, RESCUE,	SHELTER, RESCUE,
FOSTER, POUND,	FOSTER, POUND,	FOSTER, POUND,
BOTTLE BABIES,	BOTTLE BABIES,	BOTTLE BABIES,
PUREBRED LADIES,	PUREBRED LADIES,	PUREBRED LADIES,
PERFECT, DAMAGED,	PERFECT, DAMAGED,	PERFECT, DAMAGED,
ALL ARE FOUND.	ALL ARE FOUND.	ALL ARE FOUND.

(*ALL CHORUS*)
YOU WERE CLUELESS, SO WERE WE.
LESSONS LEARNED, T'WAS MEANT TO BE.
CAN'T GO BACK, REGRETS DEFINE.
BY SOME MYSTIC MASTER'S DESIGN
SHED NO TEAR, HAVE NO FEAR,
PAY IT FORWARD IN KIND.

STRAYS, the MUSICAL

(TREBLE TRIO SUNG ONCE)

BLOND OR BLUE, CALICO, CURLY, POINTED, SMOOTH, WIREHAIR, SURLY, SWEETHEART, BOLD, OR SHY THEREOF, RAINBOW PETS— WE'RE YOURS TO LOVE.	BLOND OR BLUE, CALICO, CURLY, POINTED, SMOOTH, WIREHAIR, SURLY, SWEETHEART, BOLD, OR SHY THEREOF, RAINBOW PETS— WE'RE YOURS TO LOVE.	BLOND OR BLUE, CALICO, CURLY, POINTED, SMOOTH, WIREHAIR, SURLY, SWEETHEART, BOLD, OR SHY THEREOF, RAINBOW PETS— WE'RE YOURS TO LOVE.

(ALL CHORUS)
LOVE ME NOW, LOVE ME THEN,
LOVE ME WHEN WE MEET AGAIN
AT THE BRIDGE, THE RAINBOW SHINES
BY SOME MYSTIC MASTER'S DESIGN
IN ITS LIGHT, EVER BRIGHT,
YOU WILL ALWAYS BE MINE.

(ALL! SUNG TWICE)

BLACK AND WHITE, BRINDLE OR TABBY, MERLE OR BROWN, SABLE, ABBY, PERSIAN, COLLIE, WHOLE OR FIXED, RAINBOW PETS A PERFECT MIX.	WHOOPS OR PLANNED, SHOWN OR BANNED, SHELTER, RESCUE, FOSTER, POUND, BOTTLE BABIES, PUREBRED LADIES, PERFECT, DAMAGED, ALL ARE FOUND.	BLOND OR BLUE, CALICO, CURLY, POINTED, SMOOTH, WIREHAIR, SURLY, SWEETHEART, BOLD, OR SHY THEREOF, RAINBOW PETS— WE'RE YOURS TO LOVE.
BLACK AND WHITE, BRINDLE OR TABBY, MERLE OR BROWN, SABLE, ABBY, PERSIAN, COLLIE, WHOLE OR FIXED, RAINBOW PETS A PERFECT MIX.	WHOOPS OR PLANNED, SHOWN OR BANNED, SHELTER, RESCUE, FOSTER, POUND, BOTTLE BABIES, PUREBRED LADIES, PERFECT, DAMAGED, ALL ARE FOUND.	BLOND OR BLUE, CALICO, CURLY, POINTED, SMOOTH, WIREHAIR, SURLY, SWEETHEART, BOLD, OR SHY THEREOF, RAINBOW PETS— WE'RE YOURS TO LOVE.

CURTAIN

STRAYS REPRISE (curtain call)

Suggested slide show of actors' pets projected during the song.

I WANT A HOME, SOMEONE TO LOVE.
WHEN LEFT IN THE LURCH, I WON'T EVEN THE SCORE.
FATED TO BE, IF YOU'LL JUST TAKE ME
NO MORE A STRAY
COME WHAT MAY.

I WAS A STRAY
RUNNING ON MY OWN,
LOOKIN' FOR A WAY HOME,
EACH ENDLESS DAY.

ALONG THE WAY,
SOMEONE TOOK A GLANCE,
OFFERED ME A CHANCE,
A PLACE TO STAY.

AND NOW YOU SEE
YOU BELONG TO ME.
IT WAS MEANT TO BE.
ANYTHING, I'LL DO.
ALL I CAN GIVE
I'LL LIVE THE WAY YOU LIVE.
ANYTHING I'LL FORGIVE
JUST TO BE WITH YOU.

Listen to free STRAYS Cast Recording

http://tinyurl.com/l4y8r5w

MUSICAL NUMBERS

Act 1

1. Strays (Company)………………………………………….73
2. Grazing (Basset, Trio) ………………………………..……77
3. Itchy Dog (Swagger)……………………………………….87
4. Dream Cat (Queen, Kitten)………………………….…..…90
5. Cuz I'm A Dawg-Female Version (Bluesy-Dog)…..……...…95

   Cuz I'm A Dawg-Male Version (Bluesy-Dog)………………97
6. Normal (Company)…………………………….…..………99

Act 2

7. Dog On The Run (Mutt)………………………...………..121
8. Eight Lives In Heaven (Lucky Cat, backup/descant)…….…..124
9. The Muse (Gospel Cat, Company)……………….…………130
10. Gotcha Day (Kitten, Puppy, Company)…………………..136
11. The Least Of These (Nobody's Pets, Owners, Company)………142
12. Rainbow Pets (Pariah, Trio, Company)…………………...147
13. Strays Reprise (Company)……………………….…..……156

1. STRAYS

Amy Shojai/Frank Steele

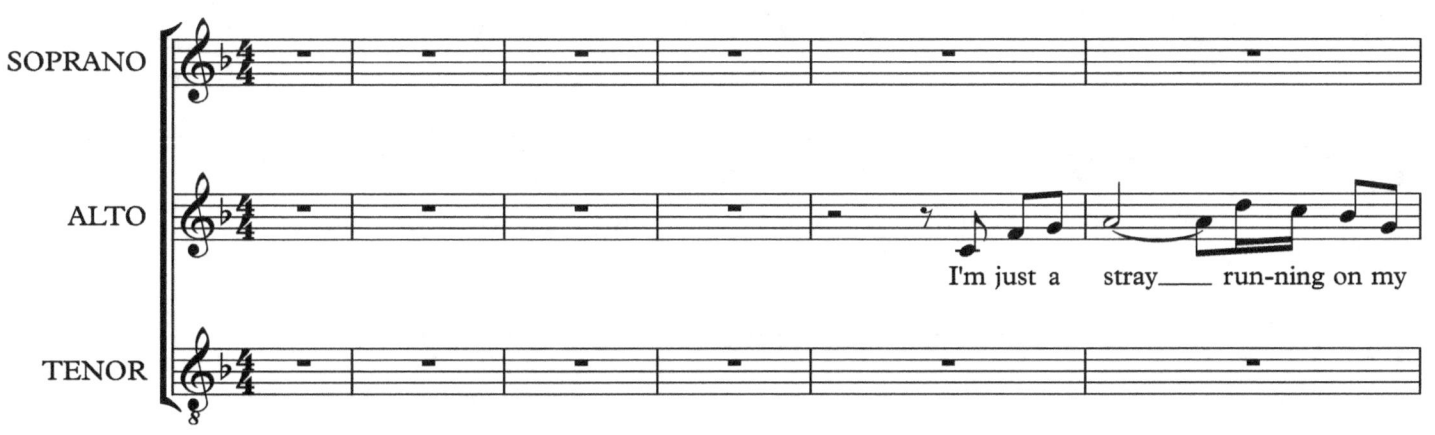

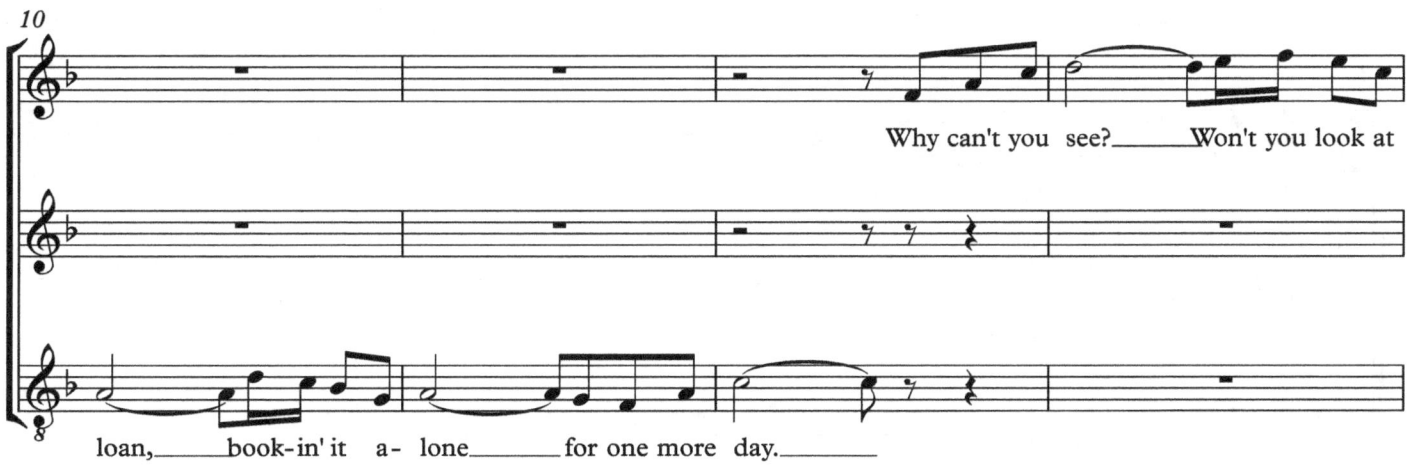

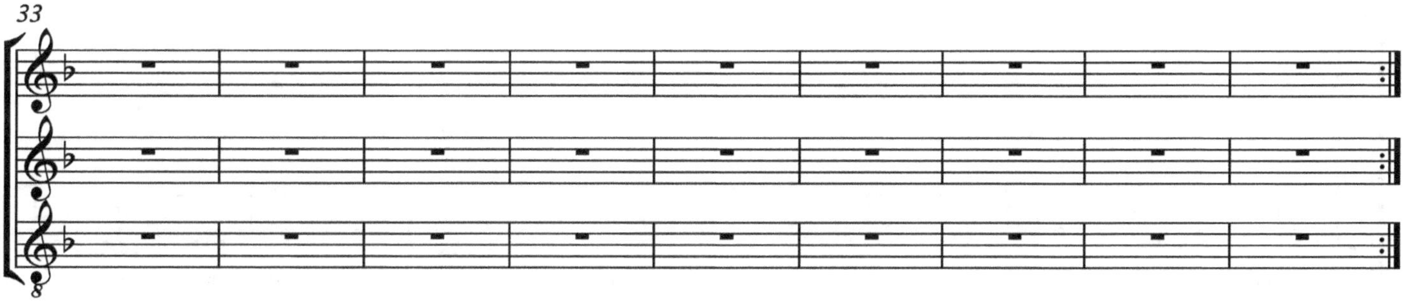

ALL: I was born to love you.
DOG 1: I'm shaggy, shorthair, big, small, and all different colors.
DOG 2: For a pat on the rump, or a scratch behind the ear, I'll do anything for you.
CAT 1: Pet me and I'll purr. Then I'll attack your hand.
CAT 2: Leave on a trip and I'll pretend it doesn't matter, and hiss to hide the hurt.
PUPPY: If you're rich, we'll live well.
KITTEN: If you're poor, we'll live day by day. But it won't matter if we're together.
DOG 1: I'll protect you to the death because I'm your dog, and I have a job to do. I'll lick clean your tears of sadness.
CAT 1: And I'll play the clown to make you smile.
CAT 2: I'll purr when I'm happy, and I'll purr when I'm hurt.
DOG 2: I'll wag my tail each and every time I see you to show how important you are to me.
KITTEN: I'm hated because I'm a cat. I'm feared because I'm a cat. I'm loved because I'm a cat.
PUPPY: The life you have chosen is my life, too. I'm not only your dog, most importantly, I'm you're friend.
CAT 1: I chose you as much as you chose me. I am your cat, and you are my person. I am a reflection of you.
ALL: We are partners for life.

2. Grazing

Frank Steele/Amy Shojai
Frank Steele/Amy Shojai

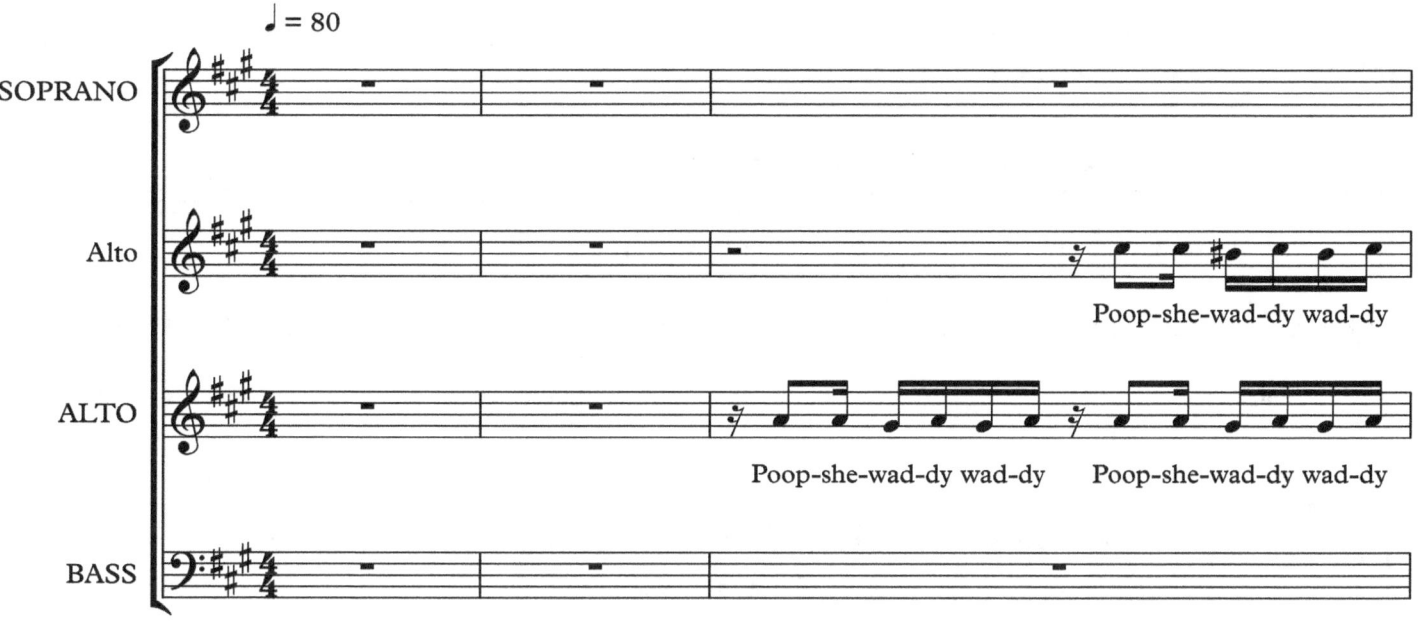

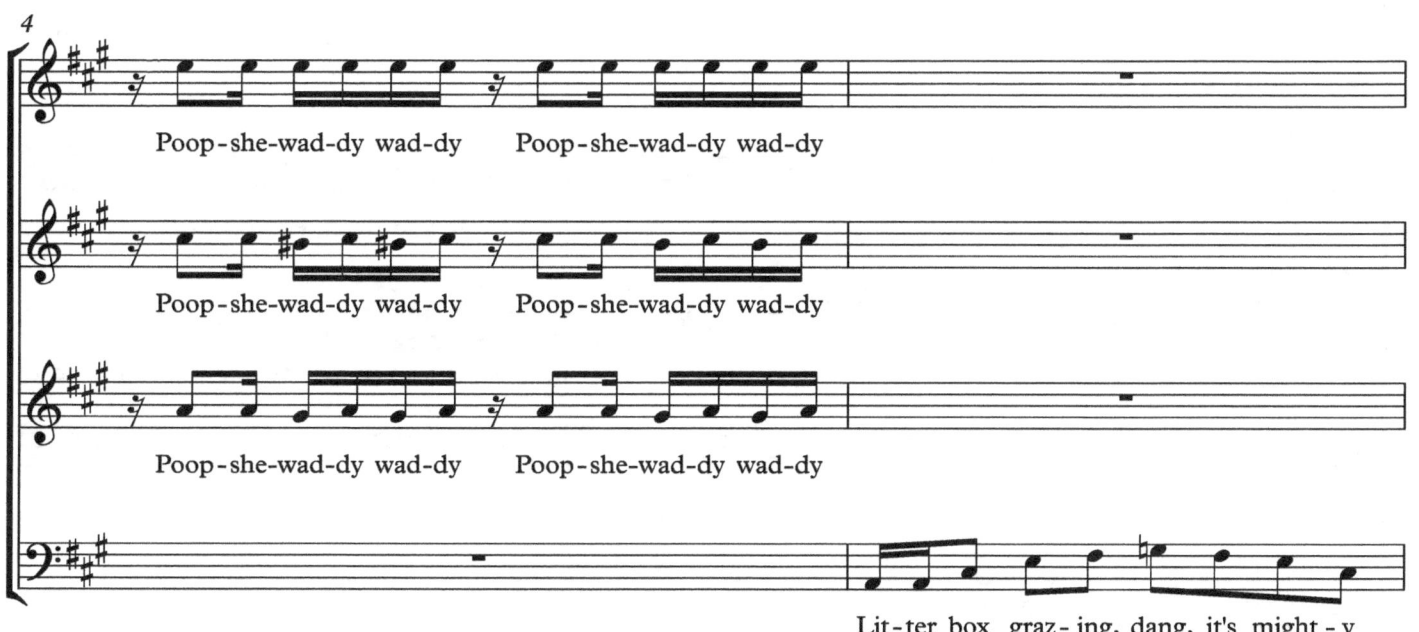

Copyright © 2013

78

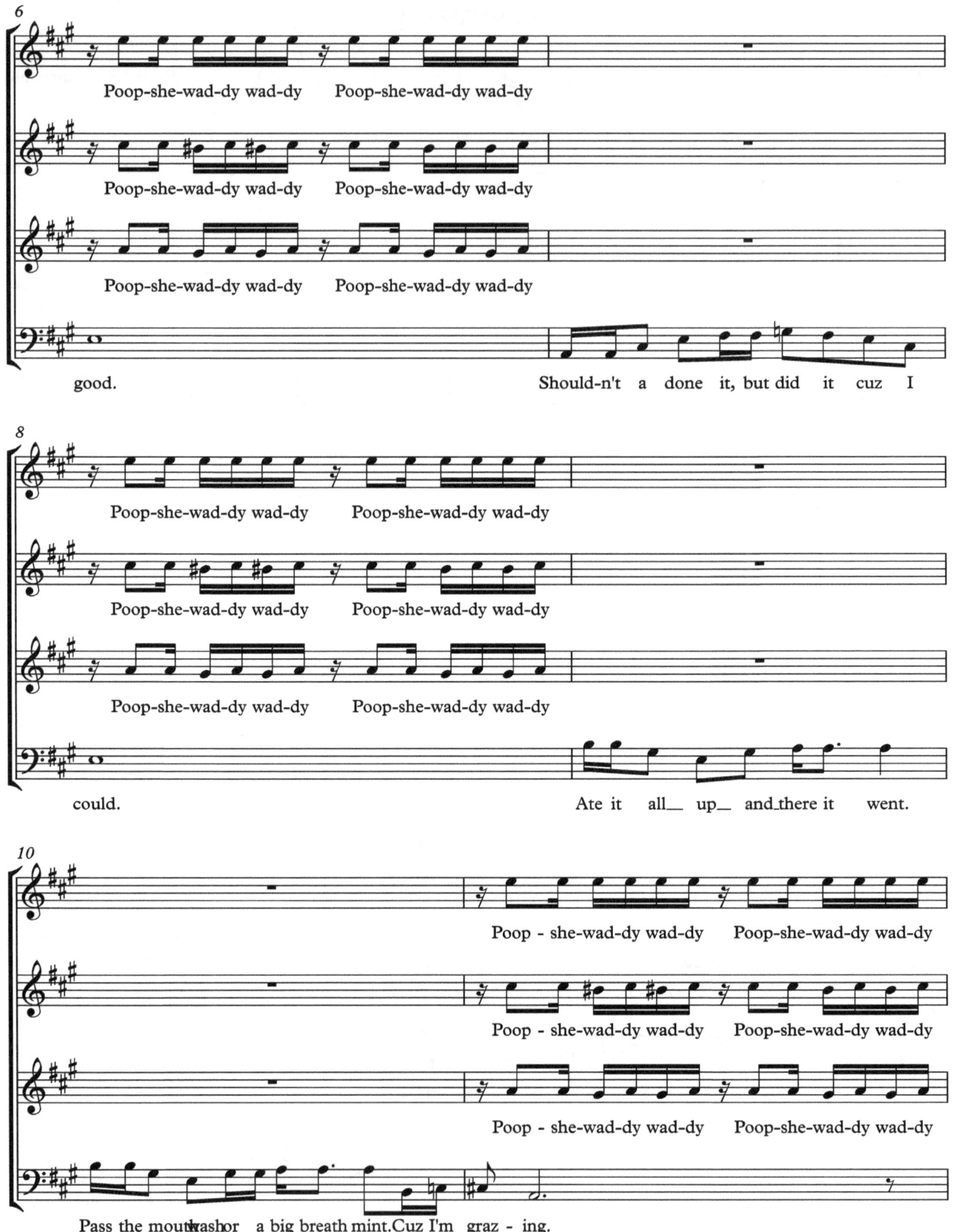

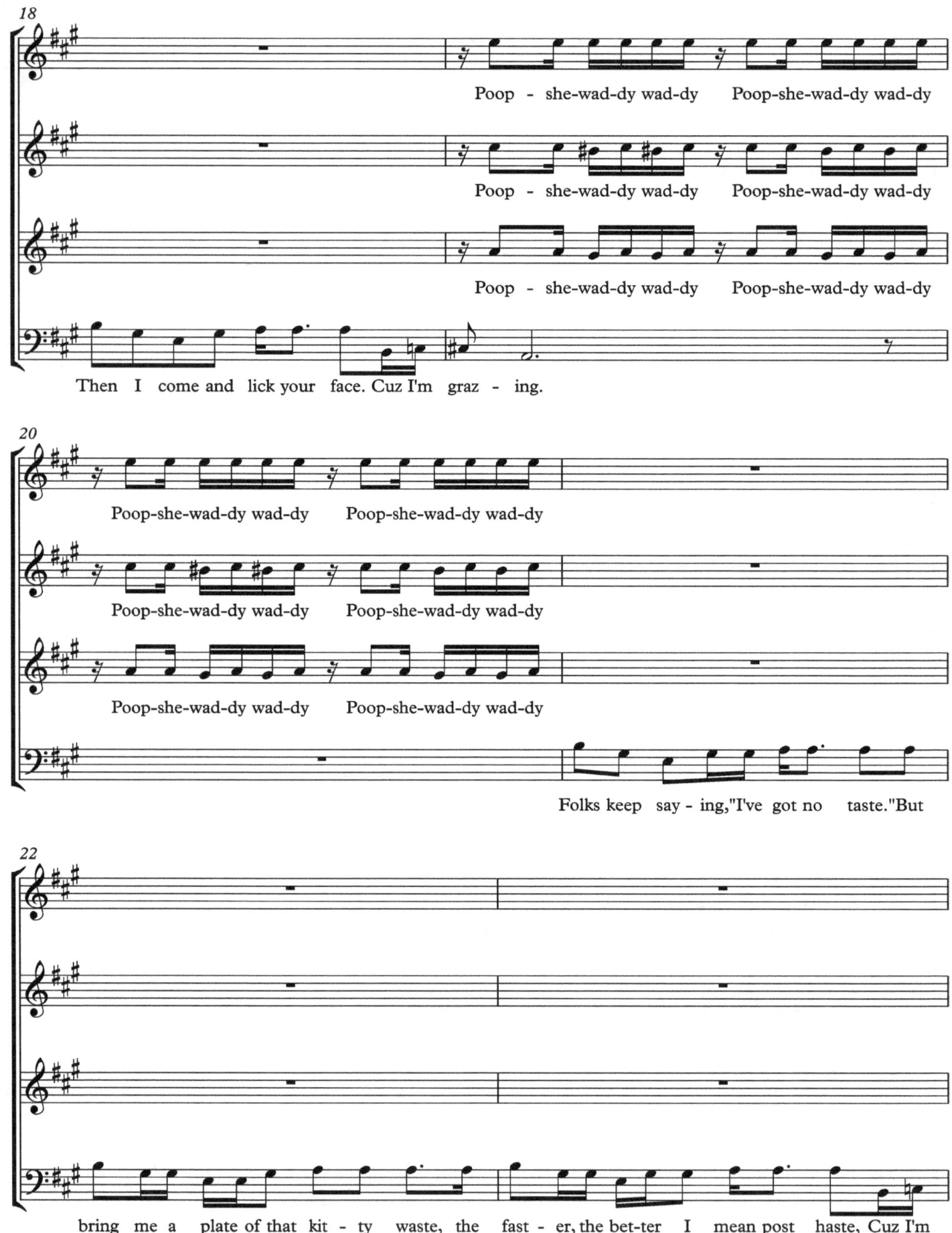

3. Itchy Dog

Frank Steele/Amy Shojai
♩ = 65

Frank Steele/Amy Shojai

I'm just a

young dog-gie on da prowl. I got new feel-in's dat make me howl. Mon, dem

hor - mones day make me itch._____ Look-in for a will - ing bitch. Tall or
(alt)hor mones that I can't hide_ Look in for a will ing bride.

short, la - dy, I don't care._____ Real - ly ug - ly, or may - be fair. Put up a

fence, Mon, and a guard. Cuz I'll be bird dog - ing in your yard.

Flip - py, dil ly, bil ly, bip py, pop. Mon, dem feel-ins don't nev - er stop.

Got dem feel-ins for da ver-y first time. How 'bout a pup, or may be nine?

Copyright © 2013

Come back to my place, I call it the Copacabana Kennel,
we have real good time. I got treats for you.

21

Yes - ter-day   I was feel- in fine.   Run-in, play- in', an oc-ca-sion-al whine.

23

Now dem feel ins got a hold on me.   Seek-in' a la-dy,   or may-be three.

25

May-be dis feel-in it go a-way.   May-be it come a-no-ther day.

27

Mon, I'll be read-y when it come a-long.   Feel-in frisk y as I sing dis song.

29

Flip-py, dil ly, bil ly, bip py, pop.   Mon, dem feel-ins don't nev-er stop.

31

Got dem feel-ins for da ver-y first time.   Don't know 'bout you, Mon, but I'm feel in fine

You heard of a lap dog, Lady? I'm a leg dog, baby!

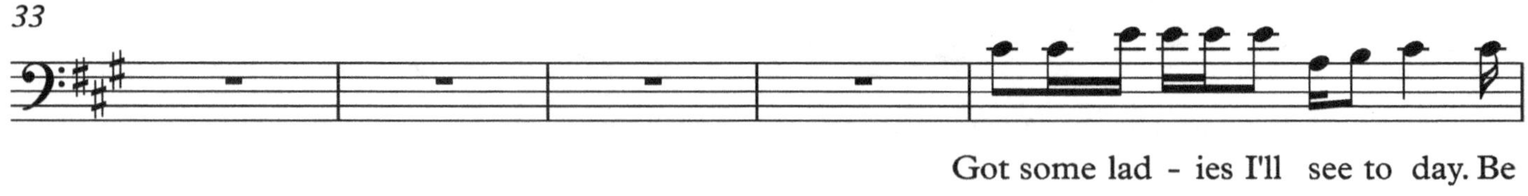

33

Got some lad - ies I'll see to day. Be

(singing) "To all the girls I've loved before..." (spoken) I used to belong to Julio Iglesius.

4. DREAM CAT

Amy Shojai/Frank Steele

Amy Shojai/Frank Steele

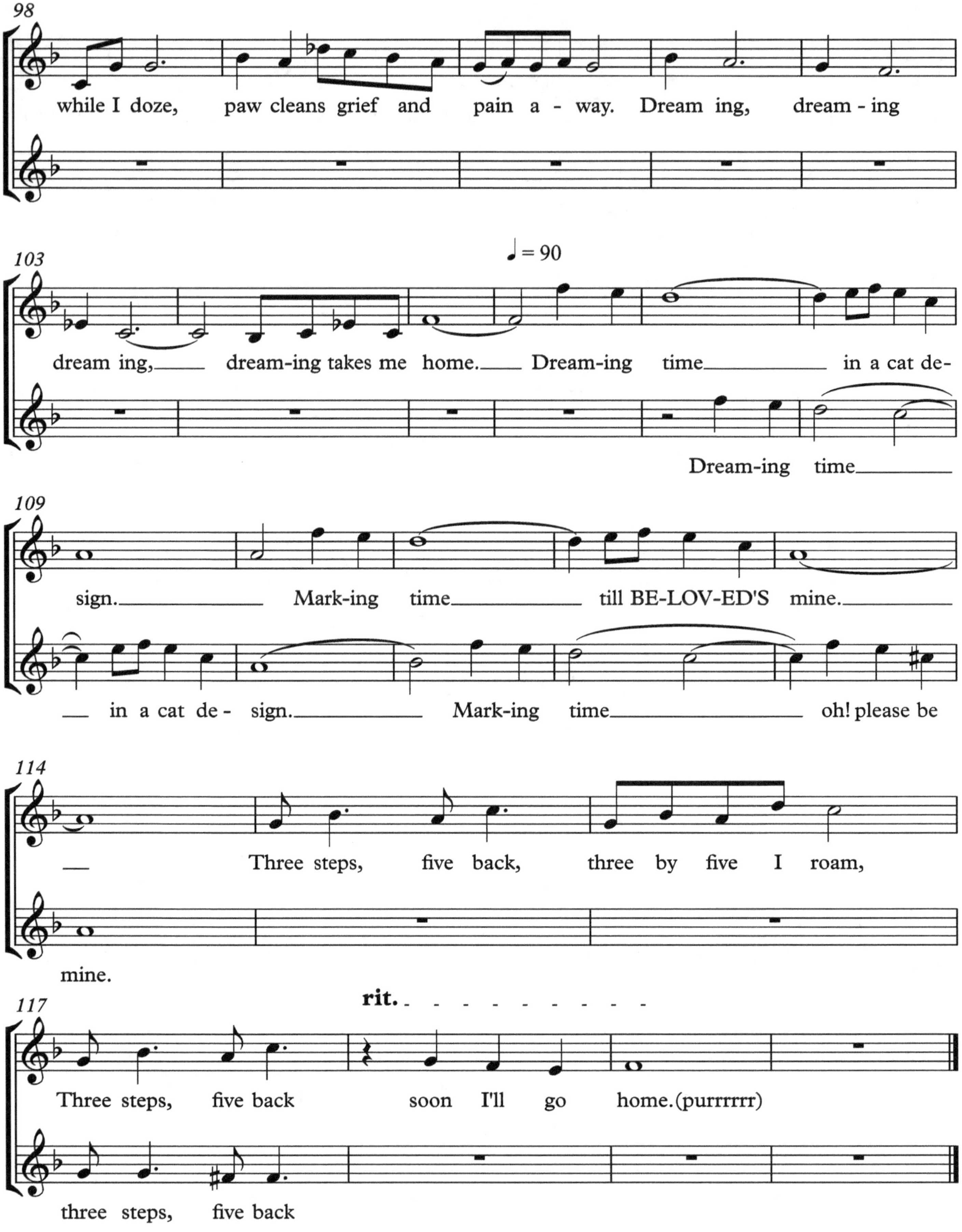
98
while I doze, paw cleans grief and pain a - way. Dream ing, dream - ing
103
♩ = 90
dream ing, dream-ing takes me home. Dream-ing time in a cat de-
Dream-ing time
109
sign. Mark-ing time till BE-LOV-ED'S mine.
in a cat de - sign. Mark-ing time oh! please be
114
Three steps, five back, three by five I roam,
mine.
117
rit.
Three steps, five back soon I'll go home.(purrrrrr)
three steps, five back

5. Cuz I'm A Dawg (Female)

Frank Steele/Amy Shojai   Frank Steele/Amy Shojai

I'll be snif-fin' you. Yes, I'll be snif-fin' you. Tell ya how it goes, wish I had Bar-bra Streis-and's nose. Cuz I'll be snif-fin' you. Gon-na wet yo' grass. Yeah, gon-na wet yo' grass. It sends my tail a-whirl, Call me da in-con-tin-ent girl. I'm gon-na wet yo' grass. Cuz I'm a dawg. A jip-jump-in' ground thump-in' dawg. I'll make a mess out-a yo' lawn, sure as da day you was bawn, cuz I'm a dawg. Got sprayed by a skunk. Yeah, got sprayed by a skunk. Get to-ma-to juice by da jug, cuz I'll be

Copyright © 2013

rub-bin' da smell on you rug. I got sprayed by a skunk. Gon-na howl all night. Yep, gon-na howl all night. It's gon-na ir-i-tate you but man, it's what I do. Gon-na howl all night. Cuz I'm a dawg. A jip-jump-in' ground thump-in' dawg. I'll knock ov-er my wat-er bowl when I'm to-tal-ly out-a con-trol, cuz I'm a dawg. Cuz I'm a dawg. A jip-jump-in' ground thump-in' dawg. I'll knock ov-er my wat-er bowl when I'm to-tal-ly out-a con-trol, cuz I'm a dawg.

5. Cuz I'm A Dawg (Male)

Frank Steele/Amy Shojai   Frank Steele/Amy Shojai

I'll be snif-fin' you. Yes, I'll be snif-fin' you. Tell ya how it goes, wish I had Bar-bra Streis-and's nose. Cuz I'll be snif-fin' you. Gon-na wet yo' trees. Yeah, gon-na wet yo' trees. It brings me lots-a joy. Call me da in-con-tin-ent boy. I'm gon-na wet yo' trees. Cuz I'm a dawg. A jip-jump-in' ground thump-in' dawg. I'll make a mess out-a yo' lawn, sure as da day you was bawn, cuz I'm a dawg. Got sprayed by a skunk. Yeah, got sprayed by a skunk.

Copyright © 2013

Get to-ma-to juice by da jug, cuz I'll be rub-bin' da smell on you rug. I got sprayed by a skunk. Gon-na howl all night. Yep, gon-na howl all night. It's gon-na ir-i-tate you but man, it's what I do. Gon-na howl all night. Cuz I'm a dawg. A jip-jump-in' ground thump-in' dawg. I'll knock ov-er my wat-er bowl when I'm to-tal-ly out-a con-trol, cuz I'm a dawg. Cuz I'm a dawg. A jip-jump-in' ground thump-in' dawg. I'll knock ov-er my wat-er bowl when I'm to-tal-ly out-a con-trol, cuz I'm a dawg.

6. Normal

Frank Steele/Amy Shojai

Amy Shojai/Frank Steele

♩ = 135

Lyrics:
Gon-na match that scratch, make my mark, mark, mark. While they snatch to catch me in the

Copyright © 2014

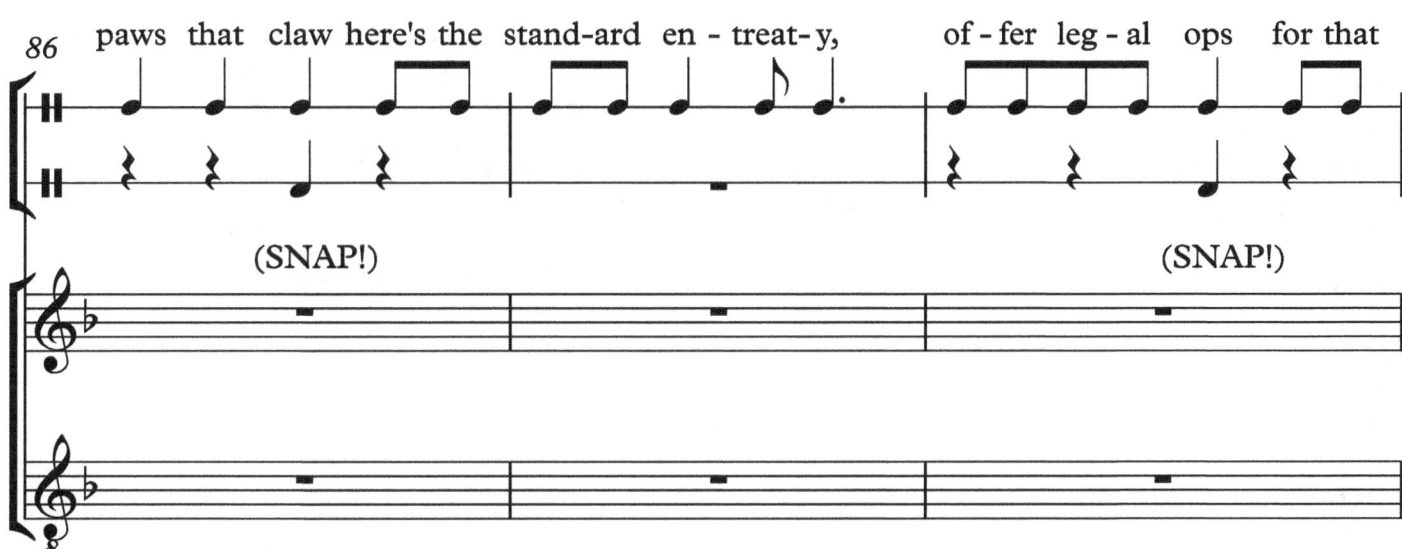
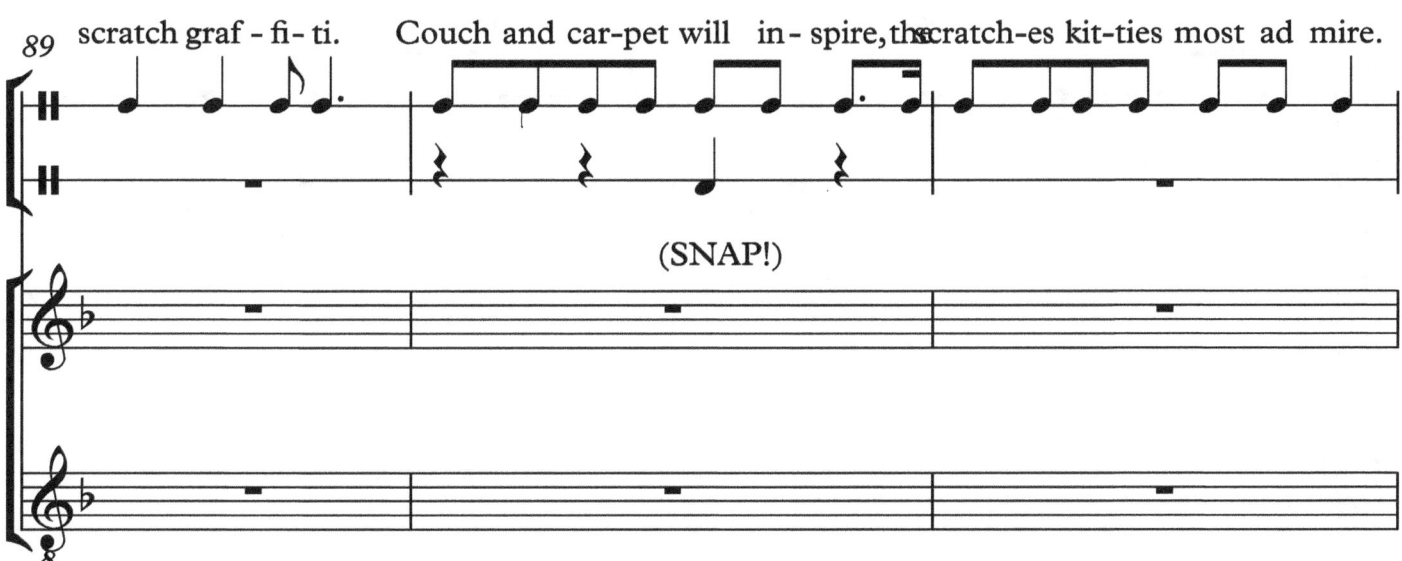

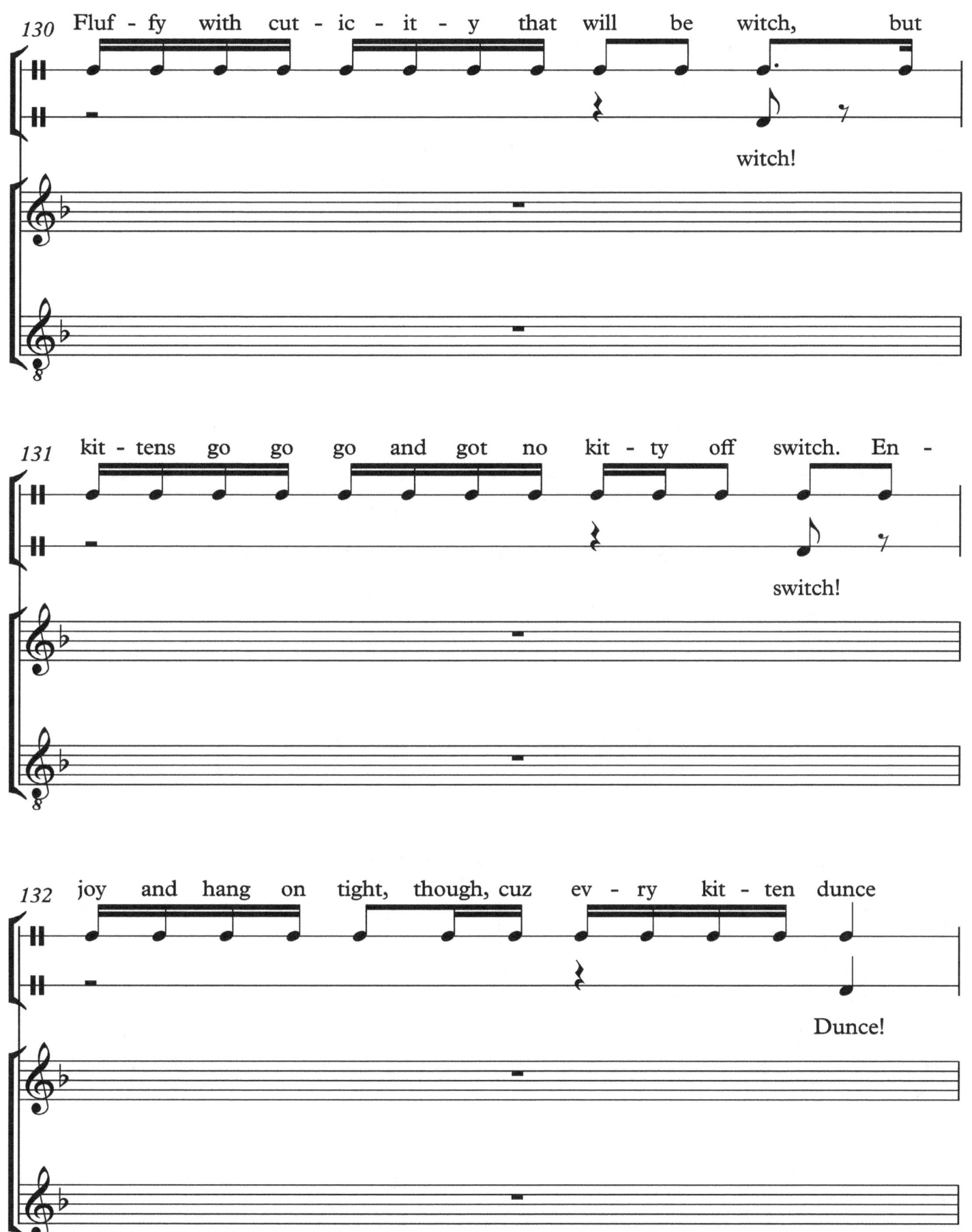

118

7. Dog On The Run

run-nin' dog, life ain't fun. Ain't no fun for a dog on the run. Pray-in' for a bet ter day,

make the bad things go a-way. Pray-in' for a bet-ter day, make the bad things go a-way.

8. Eight Lives in Heaven

Frank Steele/Amy Shojai

Frank Steele/Amy Shojai

Oooo Me-Ow___ Me-Ooo___ Me-wow.

Thought I'd im-press Miss Kit-ty La Purr by dodg-ing a ce-ment truck.

Ooooo Ooo___ Mee - Oooo_____

Oooh_____ Me-wow-ow. Meee woo ooo ooo___

Third life... not my fault... I was sleep-in' on a sec-ond floor ledge.

Me - Ow Ya - ow Me-Ooooo

wow. Meee - ow wow - wow___ Me_ Oooooo_____

What schmuck does-n't know___ to put rails on the bal-con-y

oooo.

ooo.

edge? (SING) Fourth and fifth I don't talk a - bout, you can

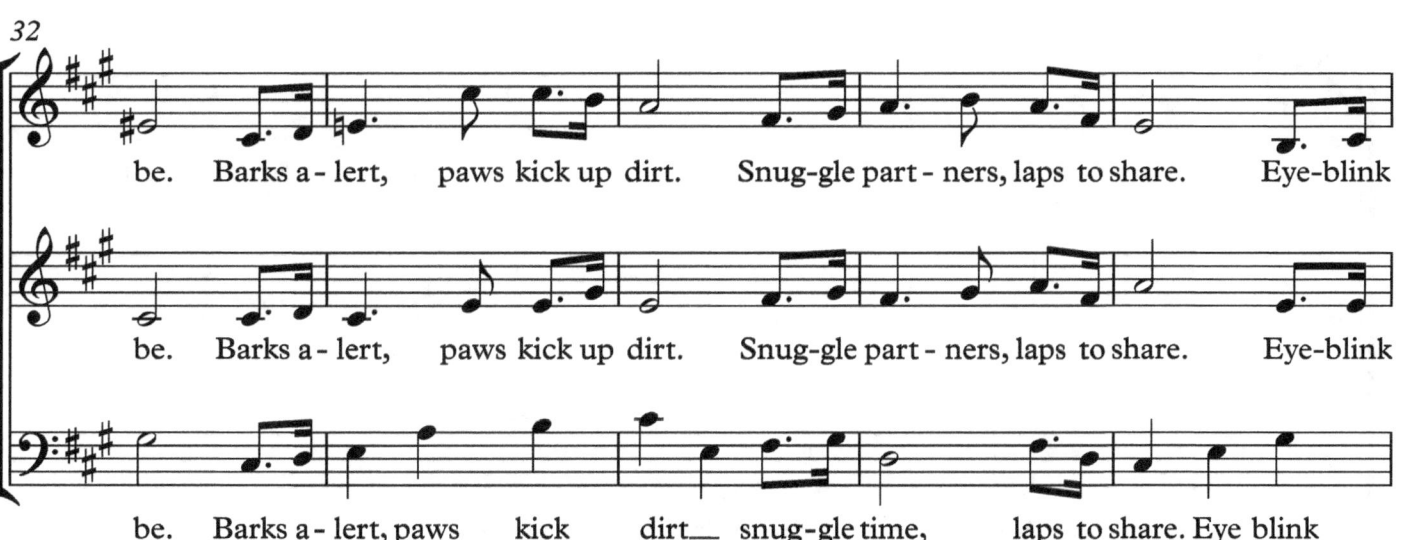

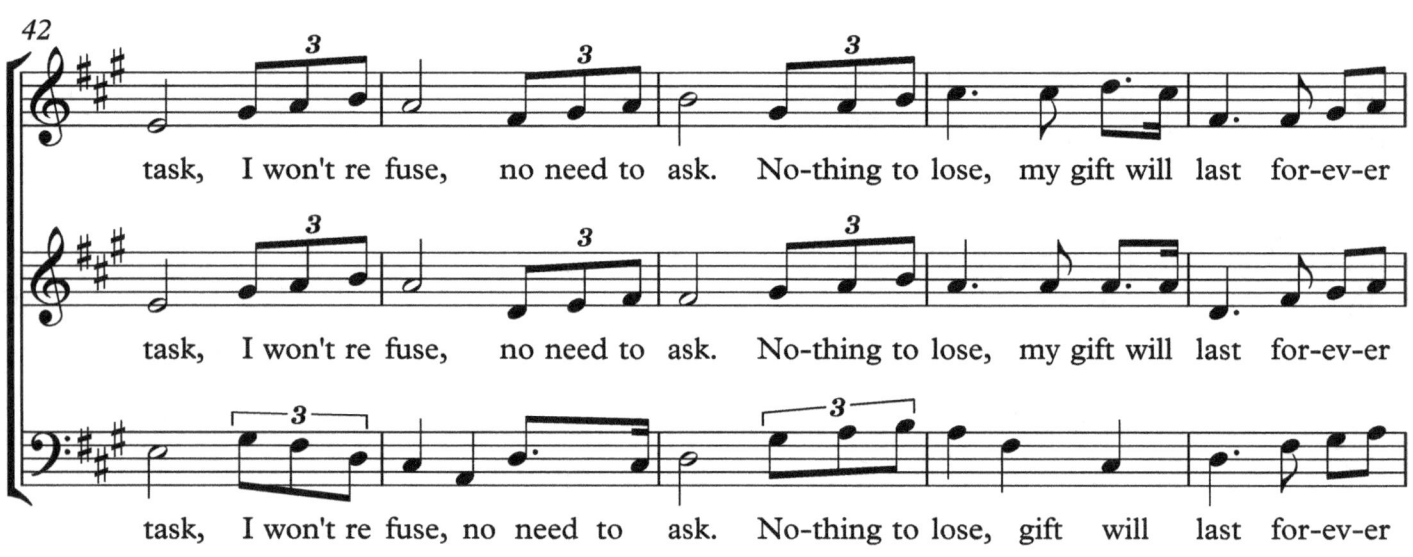
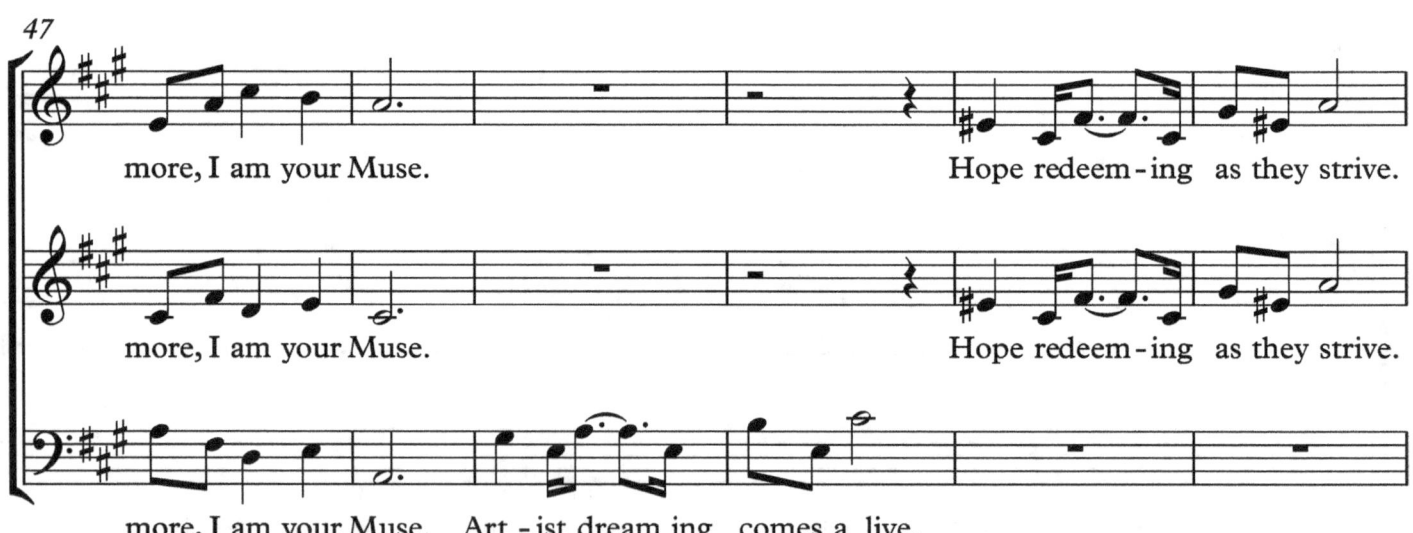

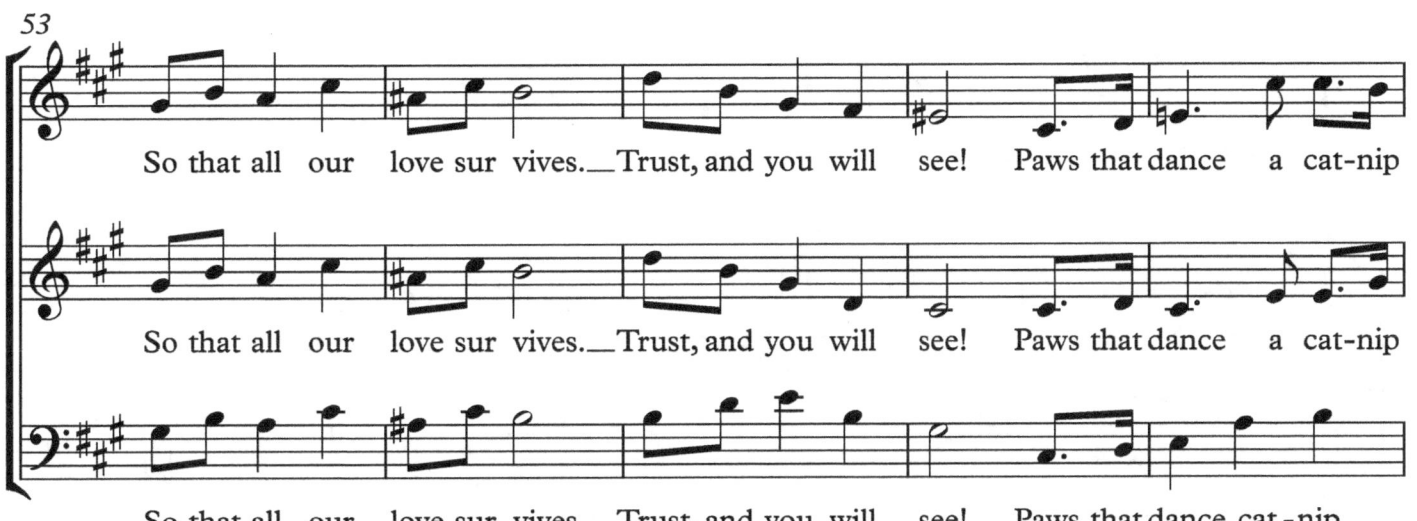
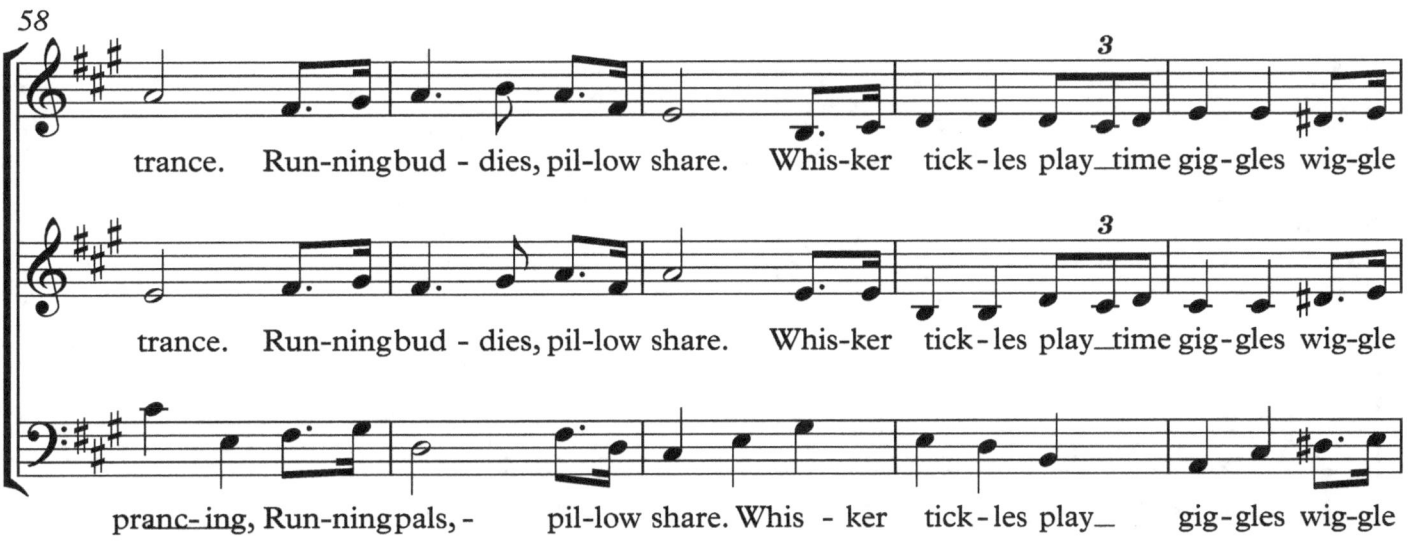
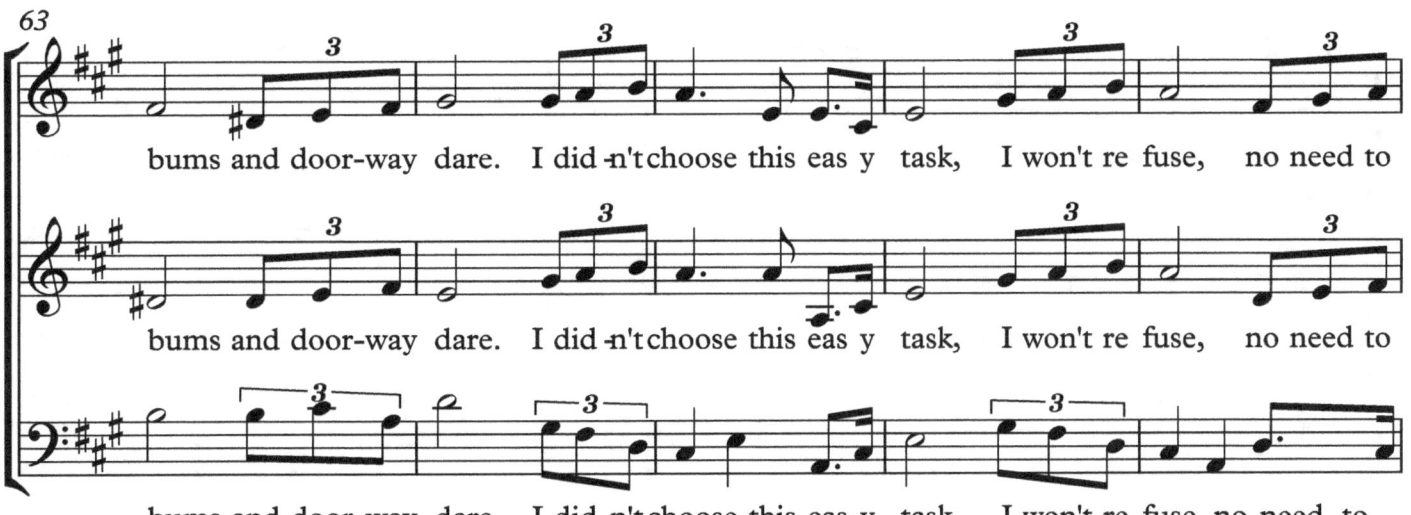

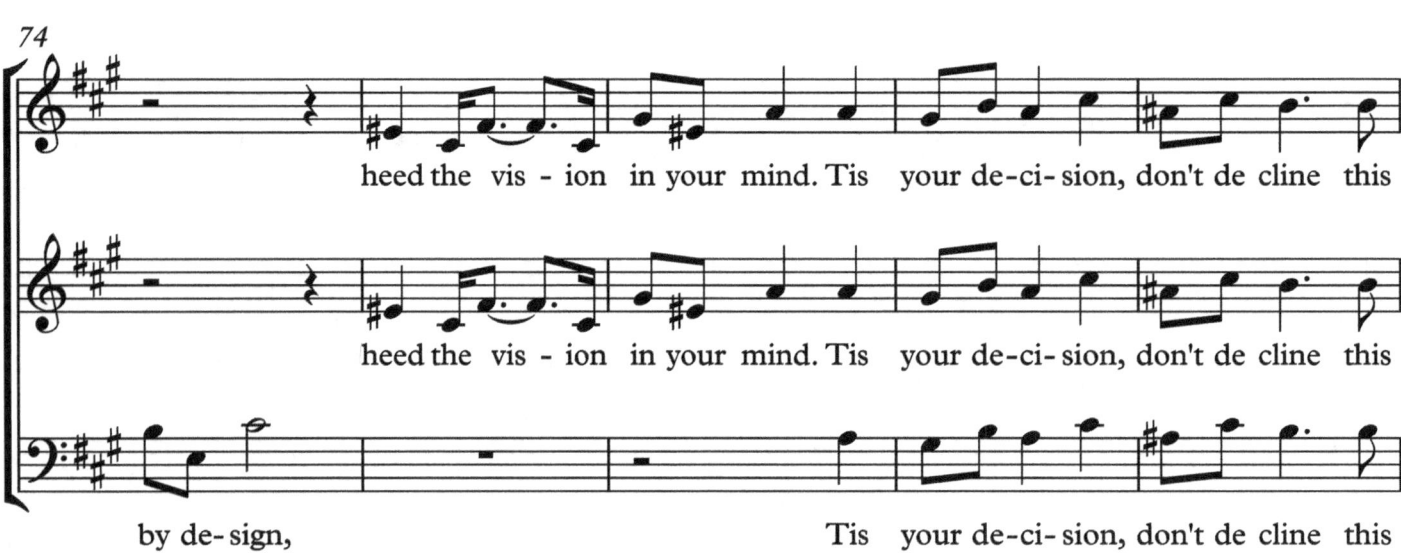
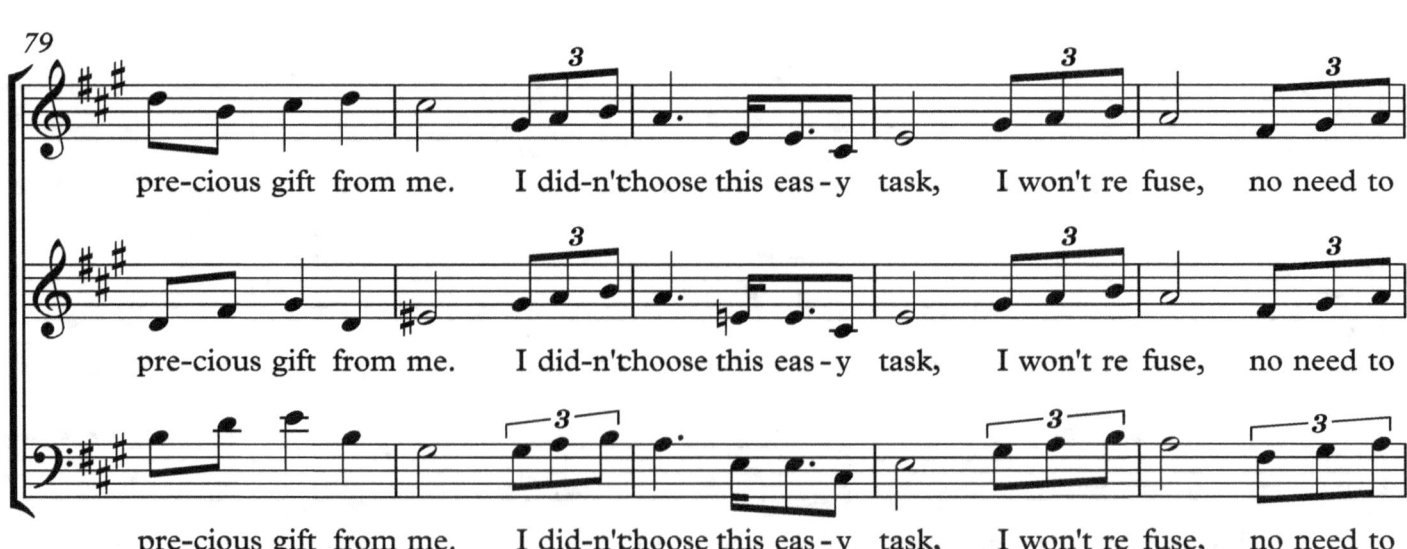

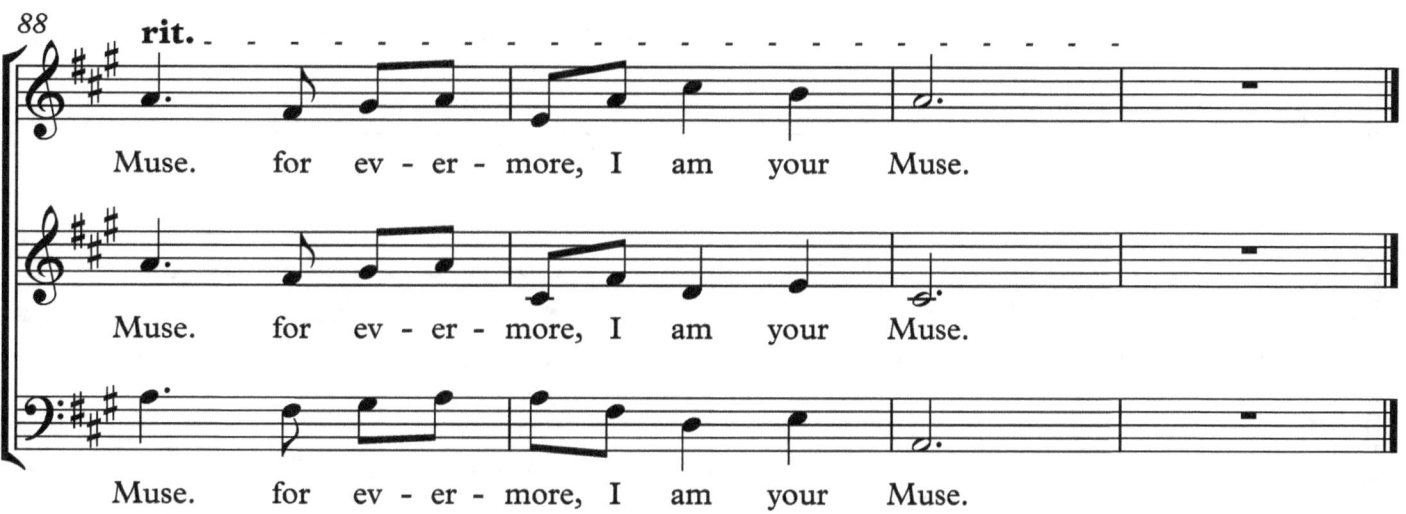

10. Gotcha Day

Amy Shojai/Frank Steele

Copyright © 2014 Amy Shojai/Frank Steele

Just look-ing, to pass the time. Not read-y. I hide my pain. Miss-ing him. But I do fine.

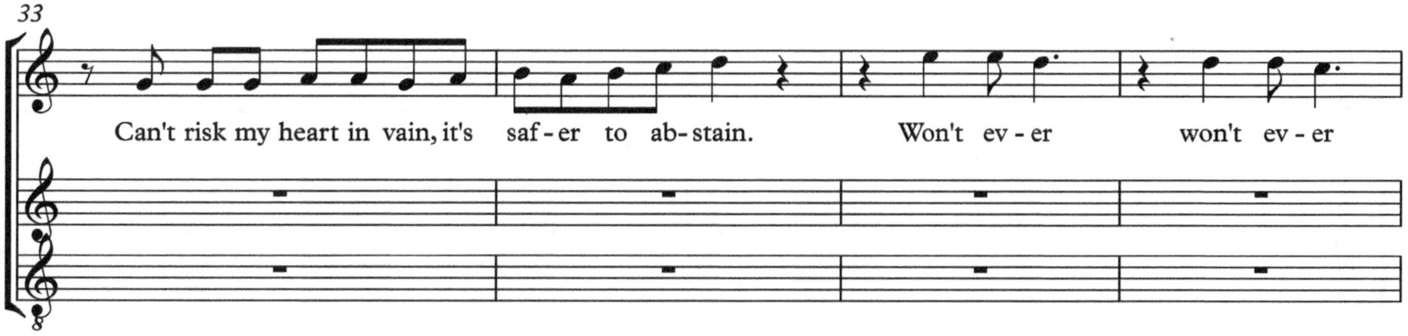

Can't risk my heart in vain, it's saf-er to ab-stain. Won't ev-er won't ev-er

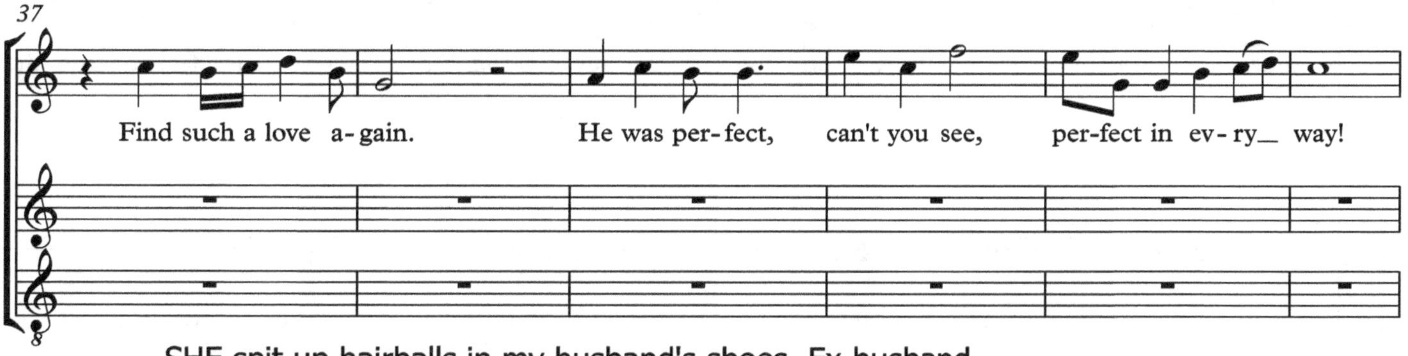

Find such a love a-gain. He was per-fect, can't you see, per-fect in ev-ry way!

SHE spit up hairballs in my husband's shoes. Ex-husband.

HE was a constant pest with that stupid tennis ball...

Just found a catnip mouse...in the silverware drawer.

It's been 6 months but there's still fur everywhere. The place is so empty now.

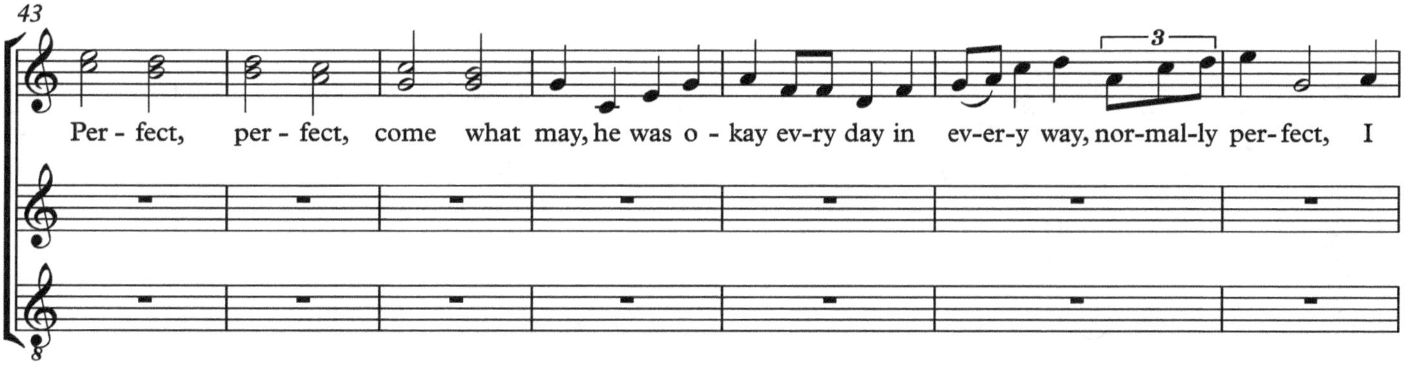

Per-fect, per-fect, come what may, he was o-kay ev'ry day in ev-'ry way, nor-mal-ly per-fect, I

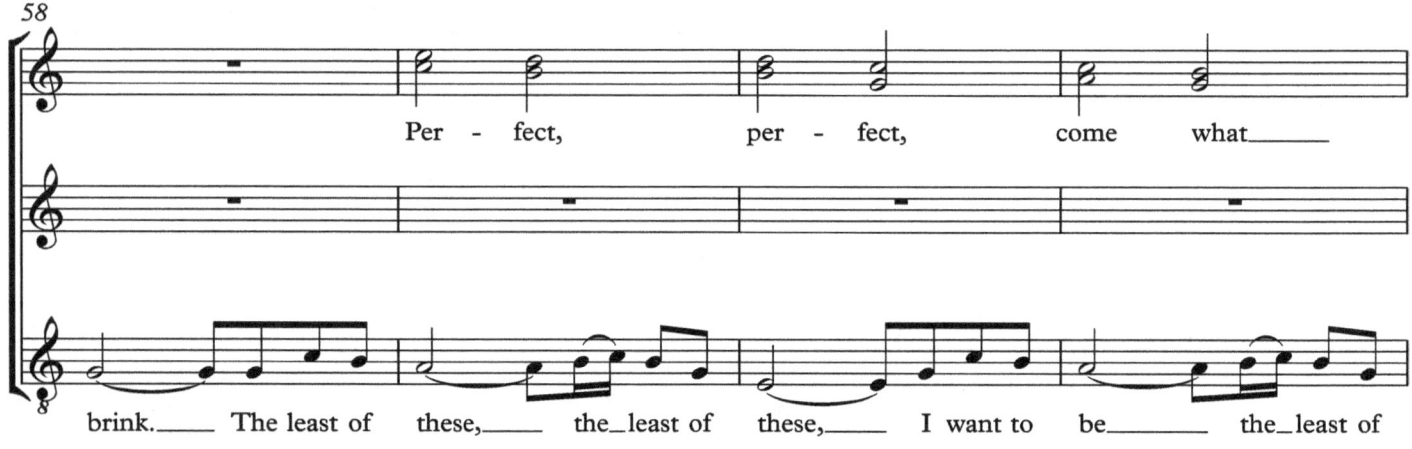

13. BOWS--STRAYS Reprise

Amy Shojai/Frank Steele

www.ingramcontent.com/pod-product-compliance
Lightning Source LLC
Chambersburg PA
CBHW081349080526
44588CB00016B/2432